"Austin Carty writes with great con_ need for pastors to be avid readers. He a\~\~ w___ and grace. The church needs this vital book."

— CORNELIUS PLANTINGA
author of *Reading for Preaching*

"The complications and tensions of pastoral ministry can make it a lonely business, both personally and intellectually. One of the most important antidotes to the perplexing loneliness of pastoral ministry is to read. Not as busywork or even distraction, but as communion with those dead and alive. All pastors need a community, obviously a community of persons, but also of authors, of people the pastor is thinking alongside, who are speaking into her or his ministry. Austin Carty is the perfect guide into this community of authors and texts. Austin is a faithful pastor who reads all sorts of texts with insight and depth. *The Pastor's Bookshelf* puts this all on display. It's a treasure."

— ANDREW ROOT
author of *The Congregation in a Secular Age:*
Keeping Sacred Time against the Speed of Modern Life

"All of us need the encouragement Austin Carty offers fellow pastors in this elegant invitation to reconsider reading. Good reading practices, he reminds us, help us preach, converse, reflect, find connections, offer lively analogies, enjoy each other, and love more richly and effectively. The book is full of stories and surprises offered with a warm collegiality that reminds us as we turn its pages of the sheer pleasure of reading a good book."

— MARILYN McENTYRE
author of *Caring for Words in a Culture of Lies*
and *Speaking Peace in a Climate of Conflict*

"Christians are a people of the Word, yet we are formed more and more today by wanton, careless words. Those who will lead the church well will be those who are formed by good words—those who know the power words have over our hearts and minds. Those who read good books well will be such leaders.

Pastors who read and live by the wisdom in this book will be changed, as will their ministries and the people to whom they minister. This book belongs on every pastor's shelf."

— KAREN SWALLOW PRIOR
author of *On Reading Well: Finding the Good Life through Great Books*

"Reading is crucial for ministry, not as a mine for anecdotes and illustrations, but as an apprenticeship of the imagination. In this warm and wise book, Austin Carty invites pastors to develop capacious reading habits, as wide and curious and wonderful as the world in which they serve. I hope this book is an occasion for many pastors to build new shelves of poetry and fiction, biography and memoir, all of them adventures in understanding humanity."

— JAMES K. A. SMITH
editor in chief of *Image* journal
author of *You Are What You Love*

"Time and again in my ministry I've been rescued from despair by a book. Partnering with novelists, poets, and scholars has stoked, funded, and fueled my ministry. Just last week Dostoevsky saved me from committing a boring sermon. That's why I so enjoyed Austin Carty's *The Pastor's Bookshelf* and found it to be full of such wonderful, wise, invigorating guidance for pastors needing to read themselves through ministry."

— WILL WILLIMON
professor of the practice of Christian ministry at Duke Divinity School
author of *Preachers Dare: Speaking for God*

The Pastor's Bookshelf

WHY READING MATTERS FOR MINISTRY

Austin Carty

WILLIAM B. EERDMANS PUBLISHING COMPANY
GRAND RAPIDS, MICHIGAN

Wm. B. Eerdmans Publishing Co.
4035 Park East Court SE, Grand Rapids, Michigan 49546
www.eerdmans.com

28 27 26 25 24 23 22   1 2 3 4 5 6 7

ISBN 978-0-8028-7910-3

Library of Congress Cataloging-in-Publication Data

Names: Carty, Austin, author.
Title: The pastor's bookshelf : why reading matters for ministry / Austin
   Carty.
Description: Grand Rapids, Michigan : William B. Eerdmans Publishing
   Company, [2022] | Includes bibliographical references and index. |
   Summary: "Encouragement and support for pastors developing a rich
   daily reading life for the sake of personal and professional formation"—
   Provided by publisher.
Identifiers: LCCN 2021043899 | ISBN 9780802879103
Subjects: LCSH: Clergy—Books and reading. | BISAC: RELIGION /
   Christian Ministry / Pastoral Resources | RELIGION / Christian
   Living / Professional Growth
Classification: LCC BV4013 .C37 2022 | DDC 253—dc23
LC record available at https://lccn.loc.gov/2021043899

This book is dedicated to
James Bennett,
Neil Dunnavant,
and Paul Sims

Dear friends,
cherished mentors,
pastor-readers
all

Contents

CONTENTS

Foreword

WHEN MY DEAR FRIEND Craig Dykstra was the vice president for religion at the Lilly Endowment, he began to be intrigued about the kinds of imagination exercised by various professionals. For example, the best lawyers, he observed, as a result of their education and their everyday working in the law, develop "a penetrating way of knowing that enables really good lawyers to notice things, understand things and do things that others of us simply cannot see or do." Dykstra named this "legal imagination."[1]

Good pastors, too, Dykstra was persuaded, develop their own way of knowing and understanding, that is, they have a "pastoral imagination." "Life lived long enough and fully enough in the pastoral office," Dykstra said, "gives rise to a way of seeing in depth and of creating new realities that is an indispensable gift to the church, to all who are members of it, and indeed to public life and to the world."[2]

In over forty years of teaching in theological schools and working with pastors in many settings, I have myself seen pastoral imagination at work. While some pastors seem to plod along mechanically in their work, filling out forms and painting by the numbers, other pastors bring to their ministries an almost artistic way of seeing people and situations, a talent for making unexpected combinations of ideas and approaches, a flair for developing creative approaches to preaching, leadership, counseling, congregational formation, and the other tasks of ministry.

Good pastors are fueled by vibrant pastoral imagination, but can it be acquired, can it be taught, or is it simply a gift that some pastors have and others do not? For a number of years, I was involved in research projects designed to find answers to these questions. Gifted and imaginative pastors were gathered into groups to read and discuss provocative books and to reflect on their ministries. The overt goal of these groups was to provide an educational forum where bright and creative pastors could learn from each other. But there was also a secondary goal, a research goal: to study these pastors themselves. We wanted to discover how their minds worked, just what constituted their pastoral imagination, and how it was that they acquired it.

We were somewhat surprised to find that these pastors, as discerning and capable as they were, were nevertheless largely unselfconscious about what they did, exactly how they did it, and where they developed the skills needed to do it. Instead of strategies and tactics, they seemed to have instead an intuitive feel for the game of ministry, and like all-star shortstops or Wimbledon tennis champs, they simply acted out of a kind of body knowledge for ministry, making the right moves and plays.

The late Senator Dale Bumpers of Arkansas used to tell the story of how a reporter at the daily newspaper in Little Rock heard a rumor that a chicken farmer near Bentonville was raising three-legged chickens. Intrigued, the reporter drove out to Bentonville to see firsthand what was happening.

"Is it true that you are raising three-legged chickens?" the reporter asked the farmer.

"Yep, thas' right," replied the farmer.

"How did you get started doing that?"

"Well, it's just my wife and my daughter and me living here," the farmer said, "and we all favor the chicken leg to eat, so I thought it made sense to see if I could raise some three-legged chickens."

"Amazing!" replied the reporter. "By the way, how do these three-legged chickens taste?"

"Well," said the farmer, scratching his chin, "I can't rightly say how they taste. We haven't been able to catch one yet."

For a long while, that's the way it was with pastoral imagination. We knew superb pastors had it, but we couldn't catch it, couldn't figure out the processes by which some pastors operated with this imaginative way of seeing life and ministry and others did not. But gradually, patterns began to emerge. Pastors with imagination, it turned out, performed certain practices and disciplines, all of which contributed to forming certain habits of mind. One of these practices was reading. Almost all of the imaginative pastors were readers, and they read not merely for pleasure or even to gain professional knowledge. They read to read; they read as a way of expanding their capacity to see, to feel, and to think.

In this innovative book, Austin Carty, himself a minister possessed of pastoral imagination, drills down deep on the act of reading by pastors. When he looks, for example, at the ministry of preaching, he argues that a steady practice of reading not only fills up the tank for preaching content but also provides "an increasingly stronger sense of what will move a congregation, and also—and more importantly—a stronger sense of *why* it will move them." Beyond this, reading is calisthenics for proclamation, an exercise of the muscles of the imagination that makes possible the angular connections of ideas and the sudden insertion of surprising images that make for engaging and extraordinary sermons.

The same is true for pastoral care, leadership, worship, discernment, and the myriad other dimensions of ministry. Carty surveys the pastoral terrain and finds the act of reading to be an enrichment everywhere. One remarkable feature of Carty's writing in this volume is how much of it is done in conversation with others, particularly parishioners and others who are on the receiving end of ministry. Carty hopes to encourage pastors who read, not merely as a form of gratuitous self-improvement, but reading done among, with, and for the people of God.

This reciprocity would not surprise Dykstra, who noted that "pastoral imagination" and "ecclesial imagination"—the imagination of the pastor and the imagination of the church—go hand in hand. In conversations with gifted pastors, Dykstra consistently was told by them "that whatever imagination and intelligence they as pastors may have, it has come to them as a gift given to them—quietly, almost unwittingly, over time—by God in and through the people of faith who make up their congregations."[3]

The good thing about many fine books is that one finishes reading them with a sense of satisfaction and completion. The good thing about this book is that readers will come to the last chsapter only to find that the task remains unfinished. Therefore, they will keep on reading and reading.

THOMAS G. LONG
Bandy Professor Emeritus of Preaching
Candler School of Theology
Emory University

Acknowledgments

Writing this book has been a dream come true for me. For giving me the opportunity, I want to thank David Bratt at Eerdmans, along with Laura Bardolph Hubers, Laurel Draper, Mike Debowski, Tom Raabe, and the rest of the Eerdmans team. Meanwhile, for getting the book *to* Eerdmans, I want to thank Neal Plantinga and Tom Long. Without Neal and Tom, this book would never have happened. For that—and for them—I will remain forever grateful.

Several friends and colleagues read early drafts of this book and offered me helpful feedback, and I owe each of them a debt of gratitude. These include James Bennett, Tommy Brown, Lucy Cauthen, Kelsey Grissom, Marshall Jolly, and Curt Lowndes. Likewise, Zach Bay, Jefferson Calico, Hulitt Gloer, Bill Leonard, and David Pacini were of great help to me in the project's conceptual stages, and I am grateful for each of them.

Through the years, both First Baptist Church of Corbin, Kentucky, and Boulevard Baptist Church of Anderson, South Carolina, have allowed me—and have encouraged me—to be a pastor-reader. I am grateful to each of these churches for their love, generosity, and support.

Finally, my children, Ada, Julianna, Witt, and Ben, daily remind me of what matters most in life, and the love of my wife, April, binds all things together in perfect harmony.

April, of all the stories I know, my favorite is the one God is telling through the life we share.

Permission to Read Freely

Many years ago, alone in my office reading Fyodor Dostoyevsky's novel *The Idiot*, I underwent a crisis of sorts. A feeling—a kind of low-grade anxiety—came upon me quite suddenly, and the longer I sat reading, the more my uneasiness intensified. The feeling grew from a slight irritation to a dull nag until finally, by the time I closed the book two hours later, a full-on sense of guilt had set in. I returned the book to my bookshelf and went about the rest of my day.

All these years later, I remember this episode as among the most pivotal and portentous moments in my life. All that follows in this book derives from this singular moment. Had I not experienced the guilt I did that day—had I not experienced such a pronounced feeling of uneasiness—I would never have given thought to all that follows.

But I did, and so I have.

I am of course not unique in having undergone a personal crisis because of Fyodor Dostoyevsky; Dostoyevsky is, after all, one of the most talented and trenchant novelists in human history. What makes my experience unique, however, is that it was not Dostoyevsky's book that made me uneasy but the fact that I was reading his book *at all*.

You see, it was 2:00 p.m. when I sat down to read that day. And I am a minister. I do not get paid to read; I get paid to *minister*. Thus, while I was being deeply affected by Dostoyevsky's prose, I none-theless felt I was being negligent in my professional duties. After all, there were members who needed to be visited, a sermon that needed to be written, a budget that needed to be balanced, and countless committees that needed to be led. Moreover, there was a building that needed maintenance, a capital campaign that needed guidance, a newsletter article that needed to be written, and two dozen emails awaiting response.

So what was I doing reading a book? And not just reading *any* book, but reading a work of fiction? I was six months into my first senior pastorate at the time, and, sitting with *The Idiot* in my hands, I suddenly found myself afraid that someone might walk into my of-fice and catch me in the act.

Ergo my crisis. I knew I could put the book up and read it later, but this was an even more daunting thought than was reading it at that time. "Later" I would be in after-hours meetings, followed by family responsibilities, followed by a (very) late dinner, followed by—before I even had a chance to catch my breath—sleep. A new day would then begin and the cycle would start anew.

And I wanted to read this book. More than that, though—and my principal reason for feeling such internal conflict—I knew that I *needed* to read this book, because I knew that reading this book was important for me. And not just important for me as a person who loves good literature, but important for me as a minister who wants to grow in my pastoral capabilities.

Though I did not yet have the research or experience to back me up, I knew in my gut that reading books—books of *all* genres—would somehow sharpen my skills as a practicing minister. I some-how knew—though I had not yet set out to study my hypothesis in any formal fashion—that reading is not just an *in*formative act but is also a deeply *for*mative act: an act that can shape a pastor-reader into a richer and more layered practitioner.

Meanwhile, I had been increasingly troubled by a growing aware-ness that, while ministers by and large profess a love for reading, very few seemed to actually take the time to *do* it. As a young minister trying to cultivate my own leadership identity, I had lately been asking seasoned ministers about their own reading habits, hopeful to find a mentor who could teach me how to integrate a love for reading into the daily practice of ministry—but I had been disheartened by their responses. *Who has the time to read,* most of these ministers had answered me, *when there is so much else to do?*

I, of course, understood their position. Being a minister is a demanding vocation, and finding margins of time can be notoriously difficult. However, I still contended that reading—no matter how busy a minister is; no matter whether the reading material has anything to do with ministry or not—could be of great vocational value.

That is why I began reading *The Idiot* that day. Determined to enhance my own vocational skill—and convinced that *not* reading would somehow limit my pastoral range—I picked the book up in fear and trembling, trusting that what I was doing was important but terrified that I may nonetheless be shirking my *real* responsibilities.

All these years later, I am glad that I trusted my instinct and pressed on that day. Today, I continue to read daily in my office, and while church members *have* inquired about what I am doing when I sit so quietly with the door closed, I no longer feel anxious or guilty about it, because I have seen my commitment to daily reading bear consistent fruit in my ministry.

Over time, as I stayed the course and began to recognize the considerable effect my reading was having on me, I began to open up to other ministers about my practice. Some of them later began coming to me—almost like Nicodemus under the cover of night—asking me to explain how reading was of "practical" benefit to me. I could sense that, just as I had that day with Dostoyevsky, these ministers also wanted to integrate reading into their daily routines but feared they could not justify the time spent. It seemed to me that they were, in essence, asking for permission to read, themselves. We *want* to read, they seemed to be saying, we just need to be able to explain how it is a practical use of our time.

3

The book you are now holding is my best attempt at such an explanation. In these pages I will share how a commitment to wide, regular
reading has practically benefited me in my own ministry, and I will
draw on similar testimonies from respected pastor-readers like Eugene Peterson, Barbara Brown Taylor, Craig Barnes, Tim Keller, Tom
Long, Fleming Rutledge, Cornelius Plantinga, and many others.

Meanwhile, I will make the case for how reading not only makes
us better pastors but also makes us better people. For that reason,
while this book is primarily aimed at vocational ministers, the lessons
are applicable to all persons interested in growing into fuller, more
enriched human beings—particularly persons interested in learning
how their faith can be deepened by an immersion in literature.

In short, over the course of these pages I will demonstrate how
reading has played an indispensable role in forming my own personal
and pastoral identity, how it has done the same for numerous other
noteworthy ministers and individuals, and, ultimately, how I believe
it can do the same for you.

The book is broken up into three sections: the first explaining what
a pastor-reader *is*, the second explaining why a pastor ought to become
one, and the third explaining how a pastor can go about doing it.

The final result, I hope, is a resource that will shine light on the
vocational value of reading while granting pastors the permission to
do it without guilt or fear. I submit this book with the deep conviction
that no minister needs to undergo a crisis like I did about whether it
is permissible to read while on the job. For, as Fyodor Dostoyevsky
says in *The Idiot*, reading is a vital resource in "the everlasting and
perpetual process of discovering."

I am just glad that I continued reading long enough to find that out.

All the Reading We Don't Remember

Reading for Formation

NOT LONG AGO I was sitting with a group of young pastors at a local coffee shop when one of the pastors asked our group what year the Korean War began.

Upon his question, a few of us at the table began hazarding educated guesses, while others pulled out their cell phones and began searching for the answer.

One of the ministers, holding up his phone, called out, "1950."

"Yes," another minister said, nodding to her own phone. "Began in June of 1950 with skirmishes along the border."

Another minister, himself reading the same Wikipedia entry, pointed out that China and the Soviet Union had backed North Korea during the war while the United States had backed South Korea.

From there, a few more tidbits of trivia were read, and the conversation was just about to draw to a close, when another minister among us, a pastor named Greg, suddenly said, "One thing that gets lost in conversations about the Korean War is the way that Korea's occupation by Japan—which was over by the time of the Korean War—fueled the antagonism between the North and the South and continued to haunt both North and South Koreans long after the Japanese were gone."

"The *Japanese*?" one of the ministers asked.

"Yes," Greg replied. "The Japanese occupied Korea for several decades in the early twentieth century—until the Allied forces pushed them out at the end of World War II."

"I don't think I ever knew that," one of the ministers said.

Nodding, Greg added, "The psychological toll was enormous. Throughout the Korean War and long after—in some cases, even still today—individual Koreans were left grappling with scars left by the Japanese occupation."

Greg went on to say more and then, wrapping up, added that, like the rest of us, he had not known the exact date the war had begun.

"How do you know all of this *other* stuff, though?" one of the ministers asked.

Greg shrugged and said, "Who knows. I'm not sure exactly. I picked up some of it from reading a novel called *Pachinko* last year that was a finalist for the National Book Award. It followed a Korean family through four generations and brought a lot about that period—and that region—to life for me."

And that was the end of the conversation.

When Greg explained how he had come about—and had been enriched by—the things he'd read in that novel, it struck me that here was a perfect example of the kind of reader I myself aspire to be, and the kind of reader this book will encourage you to be: not a pastor who reads simply in search of information, but rather a pastor-reader.

The difference is all the difference in the world, and this first section further reveals the important distinction.

1

On Formation

IN THE OPENING CHAPTER of C. S. Lewis's memoir *Surprised by Joy*, Lewis tells a story about a moment from his boyhood when he came upon a biscuit tin filled with flowers recently picked by his brother, Warnie. Years later, Lewis writes, the memory of that biscuit tin came back to him, and with the memory came a distinct sense of longing. Lewis goes on to call this sense of longing "joy," and he uses this simple image to set up the theme that will preoccupy the rest of his memoir. He then writes: "The reader who finds [this story] of no interest need read this book no further, for in a sense the central story . . . is about nothing else."[1]

I open by recalling these words because, should the story I am about to tell turn out to be of no interest, there may be no need to read this book any further, either. For, as Lewis explains of his story, so too does the story I am about to tell—simple and unexciting as it is—contain and embody the central premise of this entire book.

But in order to tell this story, I need to first tell another.

Shortly after I started seminary, I was asked by a local church to oversee a day-project for Habitat for Humanity. The project took place on a Saturday, and across the street from where we were working stood a simple, redbrick church. That morning, while pausing for a short break, I happened to see a young man—perhaps forty years old—exit the front door of a small house nearby. This young man had a Bible in his hand, and I watched him walk across the churchyard, unlock the church's front door, and then disappear inside. It was obvious to me that this young man was the church's pastor, and that the house from which he had just come was the church's parsonage.

This scene—the peacefulness of the moment, the simple elegance of the church building, the thought of the pastor praying and preparing in Saturday silence—seemed quite lovely to me. And I remember thinking, "That seems like a nice life."

Nothing more, nothing less—just: "That seems like a nice life."

Minutes later I was back to work. Soon enough, afternoon had come. And with our work now complete, we left—and I never saw that Habitat house or that little church again. But the image of the pastor walking from his house to his church stuck with me. And in the fifteen years since, I have often—without warning—found myself remembering it. And that's the end of the story.

But to understand why I tell you that story, you must understand this: At the time this happened, not only did I have little to no familiarity with small, traditional churches like the one in question but I had just spent the last half decade traveling the country as a guest speaker at various megachurches, my sense of identity predicated almost entirely on how big and how busy I could become. Thus, my conception of a "good church" at the time looked nothing like this one, and my conception of a "good life" looked nothing like the one this young pastor was living.

I would soon, of course, go on to live a similar life—and I don't doubt that my decision to do so was in some small way influenced by the impression this moment made on me—but that's not the point of the story.

The point of the story is to tell you about how I, fifteen years later, suddenly recognized *why* this moment had made such an impression on me. And to explain that, I now have to tell you another story—the one that I say encapsulates everything that is to follow.

For my birthday several years ago, some friends brought me a collection of their favorite books, and among those books was Marilynne Robinson's *Gilead*. Unbeknownst to them, *Gilead* also happens to be one of my favorites: one that I have read several times and often give as a gift to others. I thanked them for the books, put them on a shelf at home, and promptly forgot all about this new copy of *Gilead*.

Months later, though, while browsing my shelves for a different book, I came across the copy they had given me, and I decided to pull it down. My intention was not to read the whole thing but simply to reenjoy a few key passages. But after reading one page I felt compelled to read a second; and then, after that, a third; and then, before I knew it, I was set on rereading the entire thing.

Upon reflection, it had been nearly eight years since I had last read the book, and, astonishingly, over fifteen years since I had read it for the first time. And as I got about a quarter of the way into the story—the story of an aging minister reflecting on his life and ministry—I came across this passage, and it stopped me cold: "It's a plain old church . . . but I used to walk over before sunrise just to sit there and watch the light come in. I felt much at peace those mornings, praying."

And then, twenty pages later, I read this: "Perhaps that is the one thing I wish to tell you. Sometimes the visionary aspect of any particular day comes to you in the memory of it, or it opens to you over time."

And suddenly, I realized with absolute certainty something that had escaped me for fifteen years, something that time was only now "opening" to me: the reconfiguring of my life—the impetus behind my becoming the kind of pastor I had become and the kind of man that I now am—had begun through spending time in the fictional town of Gilead, Iowa, and through observing the fictional character of John Ames, *but I had never even realized it*. In other words, through that novel, a transformation had begun in me at such a deep level, and in such an unassuming way, that *I didn't even know it was happening*.

And here is the crucial point of the story: despite how readily I had cited the book as a favorite, and despite how many copies of it I had given away to others, never *once* had it occurred to me that it had played such a pivotal role in shaping who I had become.

But it had.

Had I not read *Gilead* two years before that Habitat build, and had the world Robinson created not appealed so deeply to me, there is no chance that, in seeing that young minister walk from his house to his church that day, I would have thought, "That seems like a nice life." Without *Gilead*, the internal conditions necessary for that visceral response would simply not have been possible.

—

So there's the story. And as I said in the beginning, if it does not resonate with you, or if it fails to be sufficiently compelling, the rest of this book may prove to be unhelpful as well. But before giving up on me, allow me to tell you one other story, this one about why I was even at that Habitat build to begin with.

You see, six months earlier I'd been a high school English teacher with no discernible plans of going to seminary. Still deeply desirous of fame and still deeply driven by personal ambition, I had already crashed and burned as an aspiring actor and, more recently, had published a book that, depending on one's philosophy, may or may not have made a sound as it fell out of print.

I was still receiving invitations from churches to appear as a "guest speaker," but those were drying up, and I was now uncertain not only of what I wanted to do but of who I wanted to be, and I had fallen into teaching by accident. A friend, knowing I needed a steadier job and knowing I had a degree in literature, had connected me with a local high school in need of an English teacher.

When I accepted the job, I told myself that it would be a stopgap thing, something to do while I figured out what was next. But I quickly found that I loved teaching—loved it so much that there were days when I would imagine myself doing it for thirty more years. Unfortunately, there were also days when I couldn't imagine myself doing it for thirty more minutes.

I went back and forth like that for two years, vacillating between a desire to make a career out of teaching and a desire to make a break for the door. All the while I struggled to understand the pendulous nature of what was happening; I struggled to see how I could be so enthusiastic about something one minute and so disenchanted with it the next.

But then, through this experience, I underwent the first stirrings of a "call" to ministry—and it took place on account of a Leo Tolstoy short story.

—

The story is called "The Long Exile," and, in assigning it, I assumed that my students would be only marginally interested. I was wrong. Because, as the story ended, my students were irate. The story had violated their basic belief in justice, and they weren't going to suffer it quietly.

I was stunned. We had read so many great stories together that year, yet never—not once—had my students reacted to a story the way they reacted to this one. Thus, I was taken completely off guard.

The story is about a young man named Aksinov, who is falsely accused of murder. He is quickly convicted and then sentenced to life in prison in Siberia, never to see his wife and children again. Decades later, in a twist of irony, the man who *did* commit the murder gets convicted of a crime and is sentenced to this same Siberian prison. But by the time the man ends up in prison and Aksinov has the opportunity to take revenge—something he's been fantasizing about for decades—he opts not to take it.

Instead, in an act of unthinkable mercy, Aksinov forgives the man for what he's done, and then, with tears in his eyes, says, "God will forgive you. Maybe I am a hundred times worse than you!"

Tolstoy then writes: "And at these words Aksinov's heart grew light, and the longing for home left him."

However, the real killer, dumbfounded by this act of forgiveness, utterly convicted by his own wretchedness and moved by Aksinov's act of mercy, goes the following day and confesses his guilt to the warden. And here is how the story ends: "But when the order for his release came, Aksinov was already dead."

As I said, my students were incensed. For here was a man who had lost his entire life; a man who had been separated from his family for over forty years; a man who had missed out on everything that makes life worth living—all because he'd been falsely convicted of a crime. And now, when the truth has finally come out, when justice is finally at hand, this man dies in his prison cell? What kind of justice is *this*, my students wanted to know—how could a story possibly end like *this*?

And because I wasn't prepared for this reaction, I began speaking extemporaneously about forgiveness. I began talking about what forgiveness is and about what withholding it does to a person. About how resentment can rob a person of life in the same way that prison robbed Aksinov of his. About how offering forgiveness can allow for healing in us and how offering it to others can allow for healing of their own.

My students, meanwhile, were on the edge of their seats. They suddenly began talking about grievous wrongs that had been done to them. They were honest with me about their anger and open with one another about their pain. They were not only engaged, they were inspired.

For my part, never in my life had I felt that swept up in something; never had I felt in such accord with my own deepest nature. All these years later, this moment remains difficult for me to explain, and words ultimately fail.

But what I do know for sure—and my reason for telling you about it now—is that I would not have been able to speak so knowingly about forgiveness that day had I never read books like *Les Misérables* and *Cry, the Beloved Country*, just as I would not have been able to empathize so keenly with my students' sense of injustice had I never read books such as *A Lesson before Dying* and *The Fire Next Time*.

In short, I realized that day that my love for literature was about more than just my love for a good story, and that what I had been unwittingly absorbing through literature was now drawing me toward a different and more defined sense of self. I was being *beckoned* to something, something that would soon enough reveal itself to me as a call to ministry.

And for our purposes it will suffice to say: it began with a Leo Tolstoy short story and with the sudden awareness that my commitment to wide reading had prepared me for more than just cocktail party conversation. It would be several more years, of course—and as we've seen, one more crucial book—before I'd realize what *kind* of minister I was being called to be, but literature had now started me down the road to pastoral ministry, and my life would never be the same.

So, there are two quick stories about how books have been pivotal in my own personal and pastoral formation. I offer them at the outset to try to impress upon you a critical but counterintuitive point, one upon which the rest of this book hinges: reading is far more about *form*ation than *inform*ation.

From here, this book will continue to make the case that, as pastor-readers, we don't just read to become smarter or to absorb new information (though, of course, those things can happen through reading, too), but that we instead read in order to be *changed* by our reading.

When we commit ourselves to a program of wide, regular reading, we are entrusting ourselves to a process: one that we believe will mold us, shape us, open us, *transform* us. James K. A. Smith refers to this process as "reconfiguring the very horizons of our ongoing experience," and he says it takes place at "subterranean levels of our consciousness."[2]

Another way to put this is to say that a commitment to wide, regular reading exposes us to so many new people and places and ideas and ideologies that—slowly, quietly, and continually—it enlarges our sense of the world and of what is possible. In short, reading slowly makes us *wiser*—which, as we will see in chapter 4, is not the same thing as saying it makes us more knowledgeable.

Craig Barnes, seasoned minister and president of Princeton Theological Seminary, refers to this cultivation of wisdom as the development of gravitas, of forming "a soul with enough weightiness to be attractive, like all things with gravitational pull."[3] I like this image of wisdom as gravitas because, in our current climate, where ideological tailwinds bandy us about daily, most people feel a deep and visceral attraction to those rare individuals with gravitas—that is, with the gravity to remain anchored and poised.

In fact, I submit that this capacity to remain anchored and poised in the face of an increasingly complicated and anxious world is one of the most vital things a pastor can offer his or her congregation today. And if we want to cultivate such a capacity in ourselves—that is, if we want to become pastors with this kind of gravitas—one of the most proven and effective ways to do it is by committing ourselves to a program of wide, regular reading.

Which leads me to a very quick word on the latest findings in cognitive neuroscience.

(Didn't see that coming, did you?)

—

According to Maryanne Wolf, a leading scholar in cognitive neuroscience and developmental psychology, the reading brain is not a static thing. While most of us operate as if the neural networks that allow for "deep reading" are simply *given*—that is, that once these networks are developed, they simply remain intact, waiting to be utilized when necessary—the reading brain actually operates on a use-it-or-lose-it basis. Wolf writes, "Only if we [through reading] continuously work to develop and use our complex analogical and inferential skills will the neural networks underlying them sustain our capacity to be thoughtful, critical analysts of knowledge, rather than passive consumers of information."[4]

Taken together, Wolf's books *Proust and the Squid* and *Reader, Come Home* amount to a clarion call for humankind to wake up to what we are losing when we migrate away from long-form reading. It's not just a matter of our trading Tolstoy for television or Dickens for digital media; it's a matter of our brains being rewired—being literally re-*formed*—in such a way that we become increasingly less capable of engaging complexity, thinking critically, and navigating ambiguity.

Wolf makes clear that this is not a matter of speculation. Instead, numerous empirical studies have found that "deep reading" forms neural pathways that correspond with greater capacities for empathy, patience, critical thinking, and tolerance of ambiguity, while abandonment of deep reading has been shown to alter these pathways and lead to diminishing levels of those same capacities.[5]

For our purposes, we need not go any further into these studies or deeper into the neuroscientific weeds; it is enough to say that this same design principle—this principle neuroscientists call "neuroplasticity"—works in both directions. Meaning that while it takes "years for deep reading processes to be formed," and while it requires "daily vigilance by us . . . to maintain [them]," these same pathways, once re-formed (or better: once *de*-formed), take quite some time to form back.[6]

Nicholas Carr, explaining this de-formation process in his cautionary book *The Shallows: What the Internet Is Doing to Our Brains*, a book about the way our deviation from long-form reading to digital-only reading has had the effect of making us more "shallow," writes, "The paradox of neuroplasticity . . . is that, for all the mental flexibility it gives us, it can end up locking us into 'rigid behaviors.' The chemically triggered synapses that link our neurons program us, in effect, to want to keep exercising the circuits they've formed."[7]

In other words, our reading is all the while forming us *whether we are reading or not*, and it is all the while forming us whether we *know* it or not—forming not just our perception of things and not just our capacities for virtue, but forming or de-forming the very neural pathways that make such things possible.

—

So, what does this have to do with *Gilead* or Tolstoy or the development of gravitas?

The short answer is, everything. The longer answer is that while the remainder of this book will focus on how regular reading forms a pastor in qualitative, intangible ways—ways more measurable through anecdote than analytics—it remains important to recognize that the kind of qualitative formation that I will be describing has a very quantitative correlate in the way the reading brain itself is being formed.

And to tie this all together (and to prepare us for chapter 2), one final story is called for. But before telling that story, another brief insight from James K. A. Smith. In his book *You Are What You Love: The Spiritual Power of Habit*, Smith compares the local shopping mall to a religious temple, saying that the "liturgies" involved with shopping at a mall bring to light the hidden vision of the "good life" that the religion of the mall (i.e., consumerism) is offering. "Who could resist the tangible realities of the good life so abundantly and invitingly offered [there]?" Smith writes.

Smith's point is not to demean mall shoppers or to denigrate consumer culture but to highlight how one becomes a "consumerist" in the first place. It's "not because someone comes along and offers an argument for why stuff will make us happy. We don't *think* our way into consumerism. Rather, we're covertly conscripted into a way of life because we have been *formed* . . . oriented toward a particular vision of the good life . . . and by our immersion in [this vision of the good life] we are—unwittingly—being taught what and how to love."[8]

In other words, we don't consciously *aim* to be reflections of our culture; we just absorb cultural cues that quietly form us into certain kinds of people. We don't *set out* to be "shallow"; we just wade so long in the shallows that we no longer realize that we're now light-years away from the deep end.

Which leads me to my story.

When I was a kid, I loved to read. In fact, I couldn't get enough of reading. My mom would take me to the local library, and she would allow me to check out five books at a time. I'd bring those books home, read them in a matter of days, and then we'd go right back to the library for more. Rinse and repeat. It went on this way until about midway through the sixth grade, when something very simple happened that would have an outsized influence on the next decade of my life.

One day I was called to the front of the classroom by my language arts teacher and tasked with writing several vocabulary words on the chalkboard. She would call a word out, and I would write it down. This went on for a minute or two—but then came the pivotal moment. As my teacher called out the next word, suddenly a play on that word came to me. And without thinking, I blurted the joke out and the classroom erupted.

Like, the class was in complete stitches.

And the euphoria that came over me was indescribable. The experience of making my peers laugh like that—it was a true high, something I'd never experienced in such an immediate and profound way. And what struck me about it was: it had been so simple. That is to say, my joke—it had been so silly. So *foolish*.

This, I suddenly asked myself, *this* is all it takes to get such a response? *This* is all it takes to get *that*?

What followed, then, was a complete overhaul of my personality. In a matter of weeks, I went from being the kid who read a book a day to being the kid who never read a book at all. For what I'd suddenly surmised was that it wasn't "cool" to be smart; rather, it was cool to be silly. I'd now realized that one didn't gain social currency by reading all the Nancy Drew and Hardy Boys books; one gained social currency by bombing tests and saying outlandish things in class.

And for the next decade of my life, I scarcely read a single book. Even throughout high school and my early years of college, I read only CliffsNotes and the bare minimum necessary in order to pass. The thought of reading of my own volition and for my own enjoyment—of doing that which had once been second nature to me—no longer even occurred to me.

What had happened was that, on that fateful day in sixth grade, I had caught a glimpse of a different reality—of a rival version of "the good life"—and the glimpse had appealed to me. By that point, I had already absorbed enough cultural cues about what was really "important"; about what was really valued by others; about what would make my life most significant in their eyes—and here, now, I was receiving an invitation into this more important and valuable and significant way of life.

And, as Smith says, who can resist a good life so abundantly and invitingly offered? Thus, I accepted the invitation with the zeal of a new convert, and slowly and steadily I began the process of being re-formed into an altogether different kind of person. Unbeknownst to me, so too did my reading brain slowly and steadily begin the process of being re-formed into something altogether different.

—

"The consistent strengthening of the connections among our analogical, inferential, empathic, and background knowledge processes *generalizes well beyond reading*," Wolf writes in *Reader, Come Home*. "When we learn to connect these processes over and over in our reading, it becomes *easier to apply them to our own lives, teasing apart our motives and intentions*."[9]

Later in the book, after describing her own experience taking her reading brain for granted—of having spent several years failing to read deeply and regularly—she writes of coming back to it: "After I refound my former reading self, [what] came to me is this: I read both to find fresh reason to love this world and also to leave this world behind—to enter a space where I can glimpse what lies beyond my imagination, outside my knowledge and my experience of life . . . to expand an ever truer, more beautiful understanding of the universe and to lead a life based on this vision."[10]

The books I referenced earlier, the ones that I say helped reshape my vision of the good life and helped prepare me to minister to others in more thoughtful, knowing, and nuanced ways—I only began reading those books in my midtwenties.

Between the sixth grade and that time, I had taken my reading brain for granted. And because I had, the original neural circuitry that had developed by going daily to the library slowly and steadily began to atrophy, the net result being not only that I now struggled to enjoy a long-form novel or track an argument in a complex article but that, crucially, I had grown less and less capable of perceiving the difference between a meaningful life and a shallow one. In the absence of reading, my ability to "tease apart my motives and intentions" had greatly diminished, leaving me blind to how thin and self-serving my own sense of a good life really was.

It was only through returning to books such as *Gilead* that I was able to slowly realize how much I had been missing and how different my life—and the world itself—could possibly be.

Smith has it right: no one *thinks* their way into a shallower version of reality; no one *signs up* for a counterfeit version of the good life. Instead, we are conscripted into such ways of life because of the ways that we are unwittingly being formed, because of the visions of the good life toward which we are unwittingly being oriented.

Each of the otherwise mundane stories I have thus far told you has been in service to this one central point: we are all the while being formed—at a "subterranean level"—in one way or another; all the while being quietly and unwittingly oriented toward *some* vision of the good life.

If this point indeed resonates with you and you see fit to join me for the rest of the journey, we will now begin in the following chapters to look at how a commitment to wide, regular reading can form us into more thoughtful and effective pastors, calling us—and by extension, those to whom we minister—away from counterfeit versions of the good life and deeper into the kingdom life as revealed in and by Jesus Christ.

2

Formation versus Information

ABOUT FIVE YEARS AGO I was having coffee with a local pastor, and we were discussing literature and my passion for reading. I was telling him about how vital I believe reading to be for us as ministers, and, after hearing me out, my pastor friend sighed and said, "You know, I envy your ability to read like that. I really do. For me, the main reason I don't read is because, whenever I *do* read, I don't remember any of it."

"You mean fiction or nonfiction?" I asked him.

"I mean all of it," he said. "It doesn't matter whether it's a story or a book of statistics. I spend all that time reading and then, three days later, I don't remember a bit of it." He paused and then added, "So, truth be told, it just seems like a bad use of time to me."

I sat forward and said, "But that's the point I'm trying to make. Remembering what we've read is not the most important thing about reading; instead, just *doing the reading* is what matters. *Taking the time is the whole point!*"

He smiled at me, as if to end the conversation. "Like I say," he said. "I envy your ability."

"No," I said, shaking my head. "You misunderstand. I completely share your frustration—I'm only saying that uploading information to our brains is not the main reason for reading."

I then pulled out a book from my briefcase, one I had been reading the past week and had stayed up into the wee hours of the morning grappling with and marking up. "You see this?" I asked him, putting Mircea Eliade's classic *The Sacred and the Profane* on the table between us. "I have now dedicated at least fifteen hours to this book."

"You're reading that book for *fun*?"

I chuckled and then opened the book, fanning the pages before him. "And do you see all these margin notes?"

He nodded.

"So, here's the thing," I said. "Fifteen hours and all these notes later, I can barely tell you any of what I have read."

"Seriously?"

"Seriously," I said. "Now, don't get me wrong, there are certain ideas that stay with me—but the vast majority of it? Gone."

"And it's like that with all the books you read?" he asked.

"Yep," I said.

"And yet you still keep reading and marking like that?"

I nodded. "Yes, I do. And so, what I'm trying to say is that I *agree* with you. Not remembering is incredibly frustrating. If I had a dime for each time I've wished I was Bradley Cooper from that movie— you know, the one where he takes a pill and can remember everything he's ever read?"

The pastor chuckled. "I just wish I had a dime for each time I've wished I was Bradley Cooper."

I laughed. "But my point is that I have now been doing this long enough to know that simply retaining what I read is not the real point of reading something. The *real* point of reading something is knowing that something is *happening to me* because I am doing it."

At that, the pastor looked confused. "I'm not sure I understand what that means," he said.

Just then I noticed his iPhone sitting on the table by his elbow. Pointing to it, I said, "Think about it this way. Do you ever use filters to edit your photos?"

He shrugged. "Sometimes, I guess."

24

I smiled. "But you at least understand what I mean about using the filters?"

He nodded. "Yes, of course."

"Okay, good," I said. "Well, think about it this way. Think about the original picture you take—that is, think about the image on your camera *before* you've applied any filters to it. Got that?"

He nodded.

"Okay, now think about your first iPhone and how it came with just a few filter options. Remember that?"

He nodded.

"That was pretty cool, right? Suddenly, average joes like you and me could pretend like we were professional photographers."

He laughed. "Yeah, I remember being amazed the first time I used a filter on a photo I'd just taken."

"It was an altogether different experience from having your film developed at a Walgreens, wasn't it?"

"Night and day," he said.

"Suddenly," I went on, "you had direct access to the image in question—*which remained the same image* no matter which filter you looked through—but nonetheless you now had these four or five different ways of looking at the same thing. Right?"

He nodded. "Yes—but man, that feels like a million years ago." Then, grabbing his phone and holding it up, he said, "Now I feel like I have a hundred filters on this thing."

"Exactly," I said. "And what's that like?"

"I'll admit," he said, "even though I don't use it that much, it *is* pretty amazing. Particularly when you compare it to what things were like when we used to have to go to the drug store to get a single picture developed."

—

Okay, we need to step away from this story to make a few crucial points, but I promise we will come back to it in just a moment. For now, though, I need to highlight something incredibly important:

outside of the handful of genetic lottery winners—that is, the small number of folks born with photographic memories—the best of readers only retain (on average) 10 percent of what they read.[1] Which means that, for people like me, who read at least thirty hours a week, we retain—*at best*—only three hours' worth of what we have read.

When looked at from that angle, reading really *does* look like a poor time investment. Worse still, we don't even get to choose which three hours we retain!

So, it is very important that we pay due attention and give due affirmation to the point this pastor was making. He was merely naming a frustration that we *all* experience when it comes to reading, and he was merely highlighting the fact that, given the statistical realities we face and the many demands on our time, reading can thus feel like poor time management.

But that, of course, was what *I* was trying to explain to *him*: It only feels like poor time management if we think the purpose of reading is to be *informed* by it.

And unfortunately, that *is* what most people think. The majority of people—pastors included—assume (in a kind of unexamined way) that the brain is like a computer, and that the process of reading is like the process of uploading data onto a hard drive. Here, one sees the reading act as instrumental and transactional in nature, its purpose being to store up information that is easily retrievable and repeatable. And if thirty hours' worth of reading does not yield thirty hours' worth of instantly downloadable and disseminable information, well—couldn't that time have been better spent otherwise?

Why bother if we can't *remember* any of it?

"*Exactly,*" I said to my pastor friend. "It used to be that you had the image, and that was that—no other lens to see it through. Right?"

"Go on," he said.

"But now, suddenly, you have *all* these filters to look through. It's the same image no matter which filter you're looking through—but *on account of all these different filters,* you are now able to see it in an increasingly rich way."

"So what's your point?" he asked. "Spell it all out for me; what does this have to do with reading?"

I smiled. "The point is this: the primary purpose of reading is not to be able to consciously recall what we have read; it's to constantly keep refining the lens through which we see reality."

He laughed. "'The lens through which we see reality'? I don't know, Austin. That sounds a little far-fetched to me."

I shook my head. "But the thing is: it's not. Even though we don't remember 90 percent of what we have read, it still *gets inside of us*—in ways we're unaware of and at depths we don't know we have. It still *enriches our filter*—even when we don't realize it is happening." I paused before adding, "This isn't just me talking, here. There are studies that prove this."[2]

"Maybe so," he responded, "but that still doesn't explain how it helps me become a better pastor."

I nodded. "And that's the hardest and most crucial part of the case I am making. I have to somehow demonstrate that *all the reading we don't remember* is still somehow part of—and still somehow informs—the person we bring to the pulpit and to the hospital bed."

"All the reading we don't remember?" he said.

I nodded. "Yes, all the reading we don't remember."

He put his phone into his jacket pocket and then leaned back. "Well, I'll say this. No one could ever accuse you of being unconvinced."

I took a sip of my coffee. "Perhaps I'm a little overpassionate. Some might say borderline obsessive."

He stood, checking his watch as he did. "You kidding? Never apologize for that. Like I said, I envy you for it."

We shook hands and he turned to leave. Then, motioning to the copy of *The Sacred and the Profane* still sitting on the table, he grinned and said, "Tell you what: call me whenever you find out how *that* one has enriched your filter."

We both laughed and then, moments later, he was gone.

———

Not long after that, this pastor moved to the Midwest and, a few years later, I myself moved to another state. And the truth is, I have had so many conversations like this one that I'd honestly forgotten all about it. But then, years later, I preached a sermon on Exodus 3, the story of Moses and the burning bush.

In that sermon I talked about how even though I have never seen a *literal* burning bush, I *have* had "burning bush" moments: experiences when God's presence has been clear and palpable to me. "In fact," I went on, "all day, every day bushes are aflame around us."

It wasn't to my mind a particularly literary or sophisticated sermon. In fact, if there were any evidence of my "reading" in it, I would have pointed toward my use of Elizabeth Barrett Browning's line, "Earth's crammed with heaven, and every common bush afire with God; But only he who sees takes off his shoes."

But that afternoon I received an email from a church member, a recently retired English professor, saying this: "You did a good job of helping us see the burning bush as a manifestation of a sacred event. The sermon brought back memories of my master's thesis on 'Mythological Allusions in John Donne's Secular Poetry,' written about a hundred years ago (actually in 1965). Mircea Eliade's work was an important influence on my thinking then, especially his *The Sacred and the Profane*, which I heard echoes of in your sermon."

Here it was yet again: my reading showing up in my ministry in ways of which I myself had been utterly unaware.

I'm sorry to say that I did not pick up the phone that day and call my old pastor friend as I'd promised; however, I did take off my shoes as I closed the email.

3

On Information

ABOUT THREE YEARS AGO I had back-to-back meetings with pastors who represent diametrically opposite ends of the theological spectrum. The experience was like whiplash. The first meeting, with a pastor friend who is deeply conservative (both politically and theologically), amounted to a jeremiad against the increasing liberalization of our churches and our country. The second meeting, with a pastor friend who is deeply progressive (both politically and theologically), amounted to a lament concerning the benighted nature of most self-identifying Christians.

Immediately after that second meeting ended, I rushed back to my office to join a conference call with an ecumenical group of pastors—led by yet another pastor friend—about "how to spur innovation in your church."

All this took place over the course of just four hours, and the experience felt like stepping from one universe into another (into another). Now, as I said, all three of these pastors are friends. But each of these conversations left me feeling troubled.

What bothered me, I later realized, was not only that there had been little mention of Jesus in these conversations, but also that there had been equally little humility involved. Which is to say, all these pastors seemed to take it for granted that their perspective was unassailable, that anyone who might question what they were saying was either foolish or problematic.

Now, it's important that you understand (and believe) this: Each of the individuals I spoke with that day is brilliant. Each one knows his stuff. The problem is how little each one knows *anyone else's* stuff.

Which led me to try a little experiment. Over the course of the next few months, I began paying very close attention to the things each of these pastors would say to me, and then, rather than challenge them on their points or simply accept what they were saying, I would ask where they had come by their information. My intention was less to track their sources as it was to surreptitiously track *their reading habits*.

What I found was that the conservative pastor was getting his news almost entirely from Fox News and from websites like the Daily Caller and Breitbart. And while he was indeed an avid reader, the majority of the books he had read in the last year—by his own admission—had been written by conservative pundits or popular conservative ministers. Strikingly, he told me he did not know who Thomas Friedman or Nicholas Kristof was, and he said he had never heard of either Elizabeth Bruenig or Ta-Nehisi Coates.

Meanwhile, the progressive pastor told me that he was a proud subscriber to the *New York Times* (digital subscription only), that he listened regularly to NPR, and that he liked Rachel Maddow but watched PBS more than MSNBC. He told me that he regularly went to sites like Vox, the Atlantic, and FiveThirtyEight for in-depth analysis. When I asked him about books he had recently read, he told me that he had not read nearly the number of books he would like to have read—here he cited his busyness—but that he had recently read Hillary Clinton's *Why I Lost* and Michael Wolff's *Fire and Fury*. He then told me that he did not know who Peggy Noonan or Jonah Goldberg was, and said that he'd never had any interest in reading either George Will or Thomas Sowell.

Finally, for his part, my church leadership friend told me that he no longer spends much time reading about politics or theology; instead, he now reads mainly business and leadership books. He told me that he closely follows church consultants like Michael Hyatt and Carey Nieuwhof, and that he had recently read biographies on various brand-creators like Steve Jobs and Elon Musk.

"Don't get me wrong," this friend told me. "I couldn't do what I do if I hadn't gone to seminary; but it's more important now for me to read books like these than it is to read books about politics or church history." He laughed and then said, "I mean, I still love Reinhold Niebuhr as much as anybody, but *Moral Man and Immoral Society* isn't going to help me teach pastors how to get more people through the doors."

—

In his book *The Pastor in a Secular Age: Ministry to People Who No Longer Need a God*, Andrew Root highlights something very significant. Looking at the challenges of twenty-first-century ministry through the lens of philosopher Charles Taylor, Root writes, "When the immanent frame makes divine action opaque, the pastor is always tempted to press the clay of her identity around the mold of business leader or political activist."[1]

What Root means is that once a pastor has given in to a conception of reality that sees divine action as unintelligible—as God being *at a distance* from one's daily life—the pastor then has to rethink what it means to be a pastor at all. That is, what his or her primary function is.

For our purposes, we needn't go any further in unpacking Root's argument; I simply bring Root up to highlight the two "models" he cites as pervasive in contemporary ministry: "the business leader" and "the political activist."

Now, models are a good thing. As pastors, we need models. Like all human beings, we are a metaphor-dependent people, and we need images that help us better understand who we are and better appreciate the functions we have been called to perform. (In fact, "pastor" itself is a metaphor, as it comes to us from the Latin *pastor*, for "shepherd.") So, the problem Root is touching on is not the fact of having models to live and work by but the way these models can unwittingly become rigid and self-limiting, reducing the scope of our calling and circumscribing our approaches to leadership. Highlighting this fact, Kevin Vanhoozer writes, "The metaphors [we] minister by often gain such a grip on the imagination that it becomes difficult to dislodge them. Such metaphors become pictures that hold us captive."[2]

In my experience, the two models that Root has identified are currently the most ensnaring pastoral models of all, and what often goes unnoticed about this is the way that our reading habits play a significant role in holding us captive. Touching on this point, Tim Keller claims, "When you read one thinker, you become a clone; two thinkers, you become confused; ten thinkers, you begin developing your own voice; two or three hundred thinkers, you become wise and develop your own voice."

We will return to reading's role in the development of wisdom, but now I want to highlight Keller's reason for why such wisdom is important. That is, *why* should we read "two or three hundred thinkers"?[3] We should read writers of differing perspectives, genres, and disciplines, Keller says, so that we can become more than one-dimensional thinkers. So that we can become capable of offering more than simple responses to multifaceted problems. So that we can develop more than one filter through which to interpret reality.

Keller's admonition would not be necessary, of course, if the majority of pastors were already doing this, but unfortunately, a great many pastors—extremely smart folks, just like my friends described above—read only in areas that accord with their interests and perspectives. Worse still, most of the interests and perspectives in question have been predetermined by the pastoral models they have assumed.

Thus, not only does my conservative friend read exclusively conservative material, his sermons have come to sound more like CPAC speeches than proclamations of the Christian gospel, thus leading to something of a feedback loop, a vicious cycle. Meanwhile, in the same way, not only does my progressive friend read exclusively left-leaning literature, he seems to have begun taking as much joy in leading a Republican to vote Democrat as he does in leading a sinner to Christ. As for my church leadership friend? Let's just say that I recently heard him describe his hundred-person pastoral team as his church's "human capital."

—

This is not to caricature or lampoon these pastors but to see them as *archetypes*. For we all know pastors like this, or perhaps we even see in them certain aspects of ourselves. My point here is to highlight how our approach to reading—in this case, how reading *strictly for information*—can play a significant role in defining us and keeping us bound to certain (limiting) pastoral models.

Now, please understand: I don't question these pastors' desire to read books on politics, business, or current events—in fact, the central thesis of this book is to read as widely and as curiously as one can! Neither do I fault these pastors for being drawn to texts that accord with their interests and perspectives; that's only natural.

What I question and fault is the motive behind their selection of texts and the instrumental way in which they approach their reading. What I came to realize was that my incredibly intelligent colleagues had become—to use Keller's word—"clones." They had become carbon copies of the people and ideas to whom and to which they had become overexposed. They were now reading strictly to become more informed. And not just to become more informed *in general*, but to become more informed about one specific identity or ideology.

There is no way to overstate how subtle and yet how dangerous a trap this is. Through being engaged in *this kind* of reading—that is, through committedly taking in so much heady and usable information—we can easily deceive ourselves into thinking that this is the equivalent of becoming wise; that this is the equivalent of becoming true readers; that this is essentially the same thing as being *formed* by our reading.

But it's not. Because while, yes, "doing" the reading *is* the main point of reading, still, if we read *only* to gain information—that is, if we read *only* to bolster our preexisting perspectives—then this, just like *not* reading, can become de-formational for us, too. Rather than becoming informed, we can quickly become *in*-formed.

Which is to say, reading only *one* kind of thing—and reading it only to upload readily disseminable information—can be just as stultifying for a pastor as not reading at all. It can narrow rather than widen a pastor's perspective and can quicky diminish his or her moral authority. Wolf again:

> We need to confront the reality that ... our default can be to rely on in-formation that places few demands upon thinking. More and more of us would then think we know something based on information whose source was chosen because it conforms to how and what we thought before. Thus, though we are seemingly well armed, there begins to be less and less motivation to think more deeply, much less try on views that differ from one's own. We think we know enough, that misleading mental state that lulls us into a form of passive cognitive complacency that precludes further reflection and opens wide the door for others to think for us. This is a recipe for intellectual, social, and *moral* neglect.[4]

Perhaps now would be a good time to tell you about how I rediscovered my love for reading. I told you about how I abandoned reading in middle school and picked it back up in my midtwenties, but I have not told you about how this reconversion took place. It will hardly surprise you to learn that it had to do with a book—that reading itself was the precipitating cause of my return to reading.

In this case, however, unlike with *Gilead*, what appealed to me was less a "vision of the good life" as a vision of how reading can *lead* to a good life. The book was Donald Miller's essay collection *Blue Like Jazz*. A friend had loaned me a copy, and, having recently found myself drawn to creative writing (though, oddly, not yet drawn back to reading), I decided to give the book a shot.

Well, suffice it to say: I loved it. I admired how clever Miller was as a writer, and I resonated with his life experience. I'd soon go on to write a collection of creative essays of my own, and its style and content were deeply influenced by *Blue Like Jazz*.

What I did not realize until much later, though, was how deeply influenced I had been not just by Miller's writing but also by his clear love for reading. Never in the book does Miller speak directly about his reading commitments, yet his love for literature lurks quietly at the edges of each page, tiptoeing to the center every once in a while to help reinforce a point before silently slipping back to the side. The effect of this is that, by the book's end, one has spent 240 pages with someone who views reality through the lens of literature.

I found this way of seeing things profoundly appealing, even though I did not consciously know it at the time. Which is to say, I did not finish *Blue Like Jazz* and consciously think, *Well, that does it: now I am going to become a reader!* Instead, I simply enjoyed the experience so much that I asked my same friend to recommend another book, and thus I read Anne Lamott's *Traveling Mercies*.

After that I went on to read Khaled Hosseini's *The Kite Runner*, and then Leif Enger's *Peace Like a River*, and then Audrey Niffenegger's *The Time Traveler's Wife*, and then Yann Martel's *Life of Pi*. Each of these books—it's amazing how I can still remember the sequence—was recommended to me by someone who loved literature, and with each passing book I was being drawn further into a way of life.

Then, finally—and here is where the story truly becomes my own—then, finally, I read Ha Jin's *Waiting*, a novel I found on my own in a used bookstore and the first book I ever read with pencil in hand for margin notes. This, to my mind, was my official birth as a reader, as someone who not only enjoyed to read but who now understood that, *through* reading, I was becoming a fuller, more realized person.

Pulling that book off of my shelf the other day, I found written on the penultimate page: "Peace/happiness is found in simplicity, if only we can stop pining for bigger and better." Seeing this—a note that I don't remember making—leads me to wonder whether my "reconfiguration" (as I described it earlier) had actually begun prior to *Gilead*, whether *Waiting* had been the first in a pump-priming process of sorts.

It's certainly possible.

Either way, the point is simply to say that, had it not been for the way Donald Miller's love for literature radiated from *Blue Like Jazz*, I likely never would have gotten to *Waiting* or *Gilead* at all.

⁓

So that's the story of how I came back to reading. And here is why I include it now: In revisiting *Blue Like Jazz* last week (for the first time in a decade) in preparation to write this chapter, I not only located various passages in which Miller's love for reading was obvious, but I was suddenly struck by how wide is the range of authors referenced. Just a casual glance at the book reveals such varied writers as Ernest Hemingway, Emily Dickinson, G. K. Chesterton, Douglas Coupland, Sylvia Plath, Jane Austen, Gerard Manley Hopkins, Homer, Martin Luther King Jr., and William Shakespeare. And that's just scratching the surface.

The point, of course, is that in *Blue Like Jazz* one does not find someone who reads strictly for information—that is, strictly to confirm already-formed opinions and to arm himself or herself with facts for defending those opinions. Instead, one finds someone who reads on account of curiosity and a sincere desire to be expanded, which, at least in my experience, is absolutely contagious to a reader.

Speaking of such contagiousness, Miller writes in the introductory note to *Blue Like Jazz*: "Sometimes you have to watch somebody else love something before you can love it yourself. It is as if they are showing you the way."

I suppose the present book is, among other things, a long way of my saying "Amen."

—

I have always appreciated Fleming Rutledge as a pastor and writer, but I found myself even more drawn to her the other day while listening to her on a podcast. She was being interviewed about her magisterial book *The Crucifixion*, and the interviewer asked her a question about her trademark approach to interweaving current events with orthodox theology.

In response, Rutledge acknowledged that one of the reasons her first book, *The Bible and the New York Times*, did as well as it did was because of its provocative title. She said she had later considered publishing another book under the title *The Bible and the Wall Street Journal*, just to demonstrate that she reads far more widely than any one news outlet.

After this, the interviewer pressed her to say more about her approach to using current events in her preaching, asking her whether her style was indebted to Karl Barth's philosophy that a pastor should always preach with a Bible in one hand and a newspaper in the other. Rutledge acknowledged that the gospel ought always to be pertinent to the interpretation of current affairs, but then softly pointed out that Barth's dictum was about far more than "being topical." The point, she said, was to demonstrate that the gospel of Christ has bearing on *every facet* of reality.[5]

Having grown up in a church environment in which daily affairs were kept at a remove from gospel proclamation, only to be later formed in theological circles where gospel proclamation was often *reduced* to daily affairs, I find Rutledge's balance of these things to be refreshing.

Moreover, her response—both the depth of what she said and the humility with which she said it—reaffirmed for me how indebted her perspective is to reading. Though she didn't say as much in that interview, it is evident that her entire perspective has been shaped by the breadth of what she has read: not just the essays and articles on current affairs but also the classic works of literature and theology that are regularly cited throughout her work.

Listening to Rutledge speak that day made me recall a memorable essay C. S. Lewis wrote in 1944 called "On the Reading of Old Books." In this piece, which was originally written as an introduction to Athanasius's classic, *The Incarnation of the Word of God,* Lewis writes, "Every age has its own outlook. It is especially good at seeing certain truths and especially liable to make certain mistakes. We all, therefore, need the books that will correct the characteristic mistakes of our own period. And this means the old books."

Lewis further elaborates:

> All contemporary writers share to some extent the contemporary outlook—even those, like myself, who seem most opposed to it. Nothing strikes me more when I read the controversies of past ages than the fact that both sides were usually assuming without question a good deal which we should now absolutely deny. They thought that they were as completely opposed as two sides could be, but in fact they were all the time secretly united—united with each other and against earlier and later ages—by a great mass of common assumptions. We may be sure that the characteristic assumptions of [the present period] ... lie where we have never suspected it. . . . None of us can fully escape this blindness, but we shall certainly increase it, and weaken our guard against it, if we read only modern books. The only palliative is to keep the clean sea breeze of the centuries blowing through our minds, and this can be done only by reading old books.[6]

On Information

For Lewis, it's not that the old books are somehow *better*; it's simply that they move us out of the present, with all of the present's preoccupations and presuppositions.

Taken together, Lewis, Rutledge, Miller, and Keller offer us as pastors a literary antidote to the circumscribing tendencies of the pastoral models that scholars like Root and Vanhoozer remind us can so easily ensnare.

If we will commit ourselves to a balanced reading diet that includes writers of different periods and perspectives—and if we will approach such reading with the aim of being slowly but gradually formed rather than immediately and usefully *informed*—then we will more fully and naturally grow into the original model of pastor. That model sees us as loving shepherds, caretakers tasked with guiding our flocks through besetting dangers on both the left and the right, less concerned with adding more sheep to our number than with keeping the ones entrusted to our care healthy and safe.

4

Developing Wisdom

I WROTE AN ARTICLE for a national news outlet several years ago that, once posted to Facebook, got "shared" numerous times. The piece was a reflection on how Friedrich Nietzsche's philosophy was particularly relevant to the present moment, and I was both stunned and delighted by the response it drew. Suddenly, I was receiving emails from people I'd never met, telling me how much they admired the article and saying that they were going to begin "following" me. It was a heady and eye-opening experience.

Suddenly, I realized that social media was far more than a venue for posting family pictures or airing individual opinions. I realized that because of social media's reach, a pastor in the twenty-first century had access to a megaphone the likes of which pastors in previous generations could never have dreamed. The world was not just our oyster; it was now our audience. No longer were our voices limited to our sanctuaries; we could now be heard from Seattle to Singapore if only we talked loudly enough.

Meanwhile, around this same time, I watched an unknown associate minister from a modest-sized church become an overnight sensation—and a highly recognizable name—due to the attention he received for a single controversial post. Soon thereafter, I watched the same thing happen to numerous other ministers: they'd post something provocative, and, after the post had been circulated several thousand times, their visibility as a "leader" would increase. This would lead to more provocative posts, which would then lead to more "shares," which would then lead to even higher visibility. I watched this reality steadily grow with each passing year.

Now, I could belabor the point and tell stories of pastor friends who have slowly changed their approach to ministry due to social media, but this chapter is not about social media. It's about the distinction between wisdom and knowledge, and how our reading habits can increase not only our acquisition of knowledge but also our capacity for wisdom. I only bring up social media to highlight from the top an important aspect of wisdom, which is that wisdom, by definition, is less concerned with reach than with rectitude, and less concerned with popularity than with presence.

While this may seem like a given, it is a fact that warrants particular attention, because, lest we be on guard, ministry in the twenty-first century can seduce us into trading our pastoral birthright as "wise counselors" for the lentil soup of becoming "cultural influencers."

Which leads me to a story about that Nietzsche article.

—

At the time I wrote the Nietzsche piece, I had just begun my first senior pastorate at a small church in rural Kentucky. My associate at the church was a man named Paul Sims, a celebrated music minister who, by the time I arrived, had been at the church for over twenty-five years.

It was apparent to me as soon as I began that not only did Paul have an operatic voice, but he also had immense talent for relationship building and keen instincts for institutional management. Thus, I quickly began to wonder: Why is this guy still *here*?

I'd soon enough learn the answer to this question—not to mention soon enough form one of the closest friendships of my life—

but not until much later would I come to appreciate how Paul's deep commitment to reading had direct bearing on his decision to stay in Corbin, Kentucky.

A week or two after my Nietzsche piece had been published, Paul and I were at a convention in Dallas and we were touring the site where John F. Kennedy was assassinated. At the time, with my article having just attracted the attention that it had—and after having received such edifying notes about my "prophetic voice"—I was suddenly engaged in a daily effort to write something else that would generate the same sort of response.

I'd had a dose of national attention, and it had been like a narcotic to me. In fact, this experience had been even more thrilling for me than the national attention I'd known years earlier, because thinking of oneself as a "thought leader" is far more satisfying than thinking of oneself as a reality television star.

So it was that Paul and I strolled past the Texas School Book Depository building that day, casually discussing my Nietzsche piece and talking about '60s politics and the aftermath of the Kennedy assassination.

"You know," Paul said to me, "I think that Johnson was a far more complex person than people often realize."

"Yeah?" I said.

Paul nodded. "Have you ever read Robert Caro's volumes on him?"

I told him that I had not.

"They are among the finest books I have ever read," Paul explained. He paused and added: "I think you'd do well as a pastor to read them."

"Really?" I asked. "Why is that?"

Paul reflected for a moment and then said, "Because of how well they capture the nature of ambition—how ambition can lead us to do remarkable things if channeled properly, and how it can distract us from what matters and lead us off course, if not."

And that was that.

We kept walking, and soon our conversation shifted to novels we both admired and preachers we both liked listening to.

Later that evening, alone in my hotel room with my laptop open and an idea in mind for a "hot take" on a pressing current issue, I couldn't get Paul's words out of my head. Why was I really writing this piece? I began to ask myself. Was it because I deeply cared about this particular current event? Or was it because I knew other people cared about it and I wanted them to care about me? Was my ambition being properly channeled—or was it distracting me from what really matters?

I did not have to wrestle with the question for long. I soon closed the laptop and headed to bed, and all these years later I've never written another article for a national audience.

—

Paul Sims and I would quickly develop a very special friendship, one based on a common concern for the marginalized and a shared commitment to trying to live a Christ-modeled life. Books, meanwhile, became the lingua franca between us, the language we used to express our love for one another.

My first Christmas in Kentucky I came into my office to prepare for our Christmas Eve worship service and found a copy of the newly published *SPQR*, Mary Beard's magnificent history of the Roman Empire, sitting on my desk, a bow on it and the words "Merry Christmas, Love Paul," scribbled on the inside cover.

Meanwhile, unaware that Paul would be getting me a book for Christmas, I had gotten him a book as well: Colum McCann's *Let the Great World Spin*, in which I'd written on the first page that I'd never known anyone who exemplified the faith of Corrigan, one of the book's main characters, quite like Paul.

After that, it became tacitly understood that books would be the gifts we would give one another each birthday and Christmas, each book representing more than just the book itself.

In those years we were together, Paul and I would talk for hours about novels and essay collections, scientific journalism and presidential biographies. We would rhapsodize about Kent Haruf's fictional town of Holt, Colorado, and we'd speak of the denizens of that place as if they were beloved members of our own church. These are cherished memories for me.

But the thing I remember most about the hours I spent like this with Paul is how calm and unhurried Paul always was. No matter what else Paul had going on, and no matter how stressful the situation at the church might have been, Paul was always at ease and always prepared to lend warm counsel and steady guidance.

Craig Barnes extols this capacity of people like Paul, which Barnes calls "having *gravitas*," by describing it as a spiritual attractiveness, a warm presence that draws others through a sort of gravitational pull.[1] Years later, in his book *Diary of a Pastor's Soul*, Barnes writes that those with gravitas are marked by an unhurried, unanxious nature, by a willingness to stop what they are doing and be wholly present to those who are before them.[2]

Ministers with gravitas, Barnes goes on to explain, have experienced so much of life—have known so many highs and lows, so many triumphs and tragedies, so many wins and losses, so many celebrations and heartbreaks—that their souls have over time grown larger than the bodies that contain them. They have become wizened by what they have seen and learned, filled with a kind of wisdom that radiates from them in something like groans too deep for words. Thus, ministers with gravitas, Barnes writes, exude "a holy joy, which is what makes [them] so attractive."[3]

All of which is to say that, years later, this is how I remember Paul Sims—unhurried and unanxious, ever attentive, the holy joy of his soul pulling me toward him with a quiet, inexorable force.

—

"Somehow," Eugene Peterson writes in *Under the Unpredictable Plant*, "we American pastors, without even noticing what was happening, got our vocations redefined in the terms of American careerism. We quit thinking of the parish as a location for spirituality and started thinking of it as an opportunity for advancement. . . . The moment we did that, we started thinking wrongly, for the vocation of pastor has to do with living out the implications of the word of God in community, not sailing off into the exotic seas of religion in search of fame and fortune."[4]

Elsewhere, in *The Contemplative Pastor*, Peterson grieves the way that we as ministers often fetishize our own busyness, as if the proof of our worthiness inheres in how busy we can become. "I live in a society in which crowded schedules and harassed conditions are evidence of importance," he writes, "so I develop a crowded schedule and harassed conditions. When others notice, they acknowledge my significance, and my vanity is fed."[5]

Finally, in his memoir *The Pastor*, Peterson writes of how pursuing bigness for bigness's sake is a dangerous and destructive thing for a minister. Peterson recalls a colleague who surprised him years earlier by announcing that he would soon be leaving his present church for a considerably larger one, one that was "more promising." Peterson wrote his colleague a letter that ended with these words: "Your present congregation is close to ideal in size to employ your pastoral vocation for forming Christian maturity. You talked about 'multiplying your influence.' My apprehension is that your anticipated move will diminish your vocation, not enhance it."[6]

We will return to Eugene Peterson many times in this book (for, in my opinion, he, along with the apostle Paul, is the pastor-reader par excellence), but here is why I quote Peterson at such length now: Peterson, more consistently and forcefully than any other writer or pastor I know, draws our attention to the same thing that Paul Sims, in his wizened way, was trying to draw *my* attention to that long-ago day in Dallas, which is that egoistic ambition ought to have no place in pastoral ministry, and that once we begin to equate our effectiveness as pastors with the reach of our audience or with the busyness of our calendars, we are beginning down a path that will soon enough hollow out our substance and steadily diminish our capacity for gravitas.

In short, Peterson is warning us that if we do not remain alert and aware, we might soon begin to confuse pastoral success with Facebook shares, and "having gravitas" with having legions of followers.

———

Early in my tenure at the church, Paul and I, along with our associate minister, Alex Lockridge (who is now the church's senior pastor), helped encourage the church to develop a winter relief ministry for homeless persons in the community, a ministry that quickly grew into something far larger than the three of us could have imagined. Soon we were feeding and housing as many as one hundred people per night and were responding to needs and navigating complexities that were far beyond our level of experience.

I will say more about this ministry in chapter 8, but suffice it to say here that we were suddenly standing waist-high in uncharted waters, with an altogether new population of people coming daily to our church, their appearances and their behavior not always in keeping with traditional church etiquette and mores.

Unsurprisingly, a few members of our church started complaining that they suddenly felt unsafe at the church, and that it was unseemly for us to have such individuals loitering around our property. While I loved the ministry and was proud of the difference it was making, I was growing increasingly anxious about these murmurs of discontent. It was evident that a few church members felt that we were being reckless and naïve, our vision for the ministry overly romantic, and I was aware that these individuals were quietly sowing seeds of discontent with others.

Such was the situation when I, riding with Paul on our way back from a hospital visit in Lexington, Kentucky, received a call telling me that one of the individuals from our ministry, a young man who had been wrestling with drug addiction for years and who had been regularly volunteering with our ministry to help with small upkeep assignments, had been caught smoking marijuana on the back porch of the ministry house. The church member who called to tell me this was fuming, saying that such behavior only served to confirm people's worst suspicions about our ministry, and that, were it to go insufficiently punished, it would only serve to condone the behavior and perpetuate the problem.

"He needs to be banned from the ministry," this member said to me. "Plain and simple, Austin. *Banned*."

Irate, feeling personally betrayed by this young man and utterly aghast at his brazen temerity, I hung up the phone and told Paul what had happened. After calmly hearing me out, Paul, who had himself spent untold hours taking this same young man to parole hearings and job interviews, not to mention having spent significant amounts of his own money buying groceries for him and helping him pay his deposit at a local boarding house, said to me, "Well, what are you going to do?"

I sighed. "I don't think I have a choice," I said. "They are right: if we turn a blind eye to something like this, it *does* perpetuate the problem—he doesn't learn anything from it, and it sends a message to the rest of the community that we are soft."

Paul sat quietly, staring forward as he continued to drive. Finally, he said in a calm voice, "What is wrong with being soft, Austin? Aren't we supposed to be a people of grace?"

I didn't respond. And while we soon changed the topic of conversation, both of us knew that the decision loomed large upon our return home. An hour later, we pulled into the church parking lot and headed into the building. Then, as we reached Paul's office door, he stopped and said to me: "I love you, Austin. And I know this is not an easy decision. But I encourage you to do this—before you do anything final, go reread the first pages of *Les Misérables* and think carefully about Bishop Myriel and Jean Valjean."

Which I did.

And here is how this story ends: We opted to pardon this young man, and today he continues to serve the church's winter relief ministry with honor, keeping up with his own rent payments and always quick to attribute his own rehabilitation to the kindness and grace of the church.

⌒

What does this have to do with wisdom, you ask? It has *everything* to do with wisdom. For wisdom—gravitas—is about one's capacity to discern the bigger picture; to see beyond the present moment with its immediate concerns and anxieties; to parse the difference between what seems to matter and what really matters; to distinguish between an impulsive reaction and a measured response.

In short, wisdom is not just an *aspect* of gravitas; it is the very thing that gives gravitas its sense of gravitational pull. Wisdom is the patina that gives the holy joy of the soul its ineffable shine. So much more than simple knowledge, wisdom is about being able to properly filter reality. It is about not only comprehending something but also being able to rightly interpret it. It is about not only understanding something but also knowing how to fit it into a larger picture (and then, from there, knowing how to respond to it in an appropriate way).

The reason I have dwelt so long in this chapter on the pastoral seductiveness of bigness and busyness—on the temptations of seeking attention and expanding our pastoral "reach"—is that, in pursuit of such things, our appreciation for wisdom can become diminished. In fact, it can become *disincentivized*. For wisdom—gravitas—is almost always more measured and evenhanded than mass audiences prefer because it is by nature slow to respond and unfazed by others' sense of urgency.

And here, finally, is what this has to do with reading: Reading widely and curiously—learning about new ideas and walking in unfamiliar shoes; grappling with problems we have never faced and interacting with characters of unfamiliar personalities and temperaments—over time develops gravitas in us. Through reading widely and curiously, we are not only being exposed to other people and to complex circumstances, we are in fact being *immersed* in them. When we read with open minds and charitable spirits (dispositions toward reading that we will talk about in chapter 12), we are in a very real way undergoing tragedies and triumphs with others, experiencing highs and lows with them, feeling their joys and their sorrows—not to mention all the while absorbing daily amounts of new knowledge and information that, because of the neural pathways and emotional skill sets we are building through our reading, we will soon learn to apply to our *own* lives and circumstances.

Explaining this virtue of reading, Maryanne Wolf writes: "Exemplified by the interactive dynamic that governs our deep-reading process, only the allocation of time [through reading] to our inferential and critical analytical functions can transform the information we read into knowledge that can be consolidated in our memory. Only this internalized knowledge, in turn, will allow us to draw analogies and inferences from new information [i.e., execute wise judgment]." She goes on to say, "The perquisite of the reading life is the ability to transform information into knowledge and knowledge into wisdom."[7]

This tracks with *New York Times* columnist David Brooks, who writes in a memorable column: "People who have a wealth of analogies in their minds can think more precisely than those with few analogies. If you go through [life] without reading . . . you will be cheated out of a great repertoire of comparisons."[8]

Practically speaking, then, what this means is that, through reading, we develop the capacity to connect a difficult dilemma concerning a young man smoking pot with a difficult dilemma about a fictional French silver thief—just as it means that, through reading, we learn how to carefully caution a colleague about the dangers of ambition by citing Robert Caro books instead of by telling him to give it a rest with his Friedrich Nietzsche articles.

—

At the end of her classic novel *Middlemarch*, a book about the mundane affairs of a small English town in the 1830s, George Eliot writes:

"The effect of her being on those around her was incalculably diffusive, for the growing good of the world is partly dependent on unhistoric acts, and that things are not so ill with you and me as they might have been is half owing to the number who lived faithfully a hidden life and rest in unvisited tombs."[9]

Paul Sims's effect on those around him has been incalculably diffusive—and at least for my part, I know that it is because of Paul that things are not so ill with me as they might otherwise have been.

Just recently I found the first gift he ever gave me, a hardbound, pocket-sized 1929 literature anthology called *Great Companions*, and upon opening it, I found these words: "To a reader there is continually open the society of the wisest of earth. This volume may give the reader inspiration of such association."

"Yes, it does," I thought, feeling close to my old friend once more. "Yes, it most certainly does."

5

Learning to Love

DURING THE EXPLOSIVE SUMMER OF 2020, as the COVID-19 crisis raged on and as social tensions reached a boiling point, I, like many in the United States, found myself despairing over the state of things and desiring to be part of meaningful change. Riots and protests were occurring all over the nation, and news programs and social media were being daily flooded with images of violence and unrest.

In response to this, I called my friend Ankoma Anderson, pastor of an African American church in my hometown and president of the local African American ministerial organization. I told Ankoma that if he were open to it, I would love to partner with him to host a prayer vigil, a worship event that would bring the community together to confront the reality of injustice and to pray for a peaceful and productive way forward.

Ankoma was gracious, and he and I had a nice conversation, dreaming together of what such an event might look like. Within a matter of hours, we had spoken with our county commissioner and had secured the Civic Center parking lot for a venue. Now, all we needed was an event outline. We ended that day by agreeing that each of us would put together some notes for the service and that we would split the responsibilities of contacting local officials.

I hung up the phone filled with anxiety, aware that I had started a ball rolling that would no doubt attract far more attention and publicity than I was ready for. Thus, I spent the evening working feverishly on an order of worship, going far beyond just "making notes." I was meticulous in my consideration of each detail, staying up late into the night parsing each potential part. Who should do the words of welcome and who the benediction? Who should offer the invocation and who should lead the prayers of the people? I labored over the liturgy, trying to craft a responsive prayer that, while offered in the first-person plural, was appropriately sensitive to everyone.

Finally satisfied with my product, I emailed the draft to Ankoma and headed to bed, eager to know how he would receive it.

———

In Miroslav Volf's *Exclusion and Embrace*, the story of Abraham's journey away from his father's home to "a land that I will show you" in Genesis 11 is emblematic. Commitment to Judeo-Christian faith, Volf writes, requires a similar journey to Abraham's, a willingness to leave one's comfort zone and go places one has never been and engage people and ideas with which one is not familiar.

"To respond to the call of God means to make an exodus," Volf writes, "to start a voyage, to become a stranger." In that way, "Departure is part and parcel of Christian identity."[1]

This no doubt rings true. As Christians, we are not to hide our lights under a bushel; we are to follow the gospel to the ends of the earth, sharing it with Jew and gentile alike.

The complication, of course, is that not all of us have sufficient opportunities to "depart." Many of us would welcome the opportunity to live like cultural anthropologists or governmental ambassadors, living for years at a time in foreign locations. But for most of us, this is not our reality. Instead, the vast majority of us are tethered to one place due to the demands of work or commitment or circumstance.

This being the case, how can we affirm Volf's point without maxing out our credit cards and leaving behind responsibilities we cannot afford to neglect? How can we, as committed persons of faith, follow the paradigmatic journey of Abraham and depart our comfort zones without actually departing?

Anticipating this question, Volf goes on to say that, because of the universal scope of the Christian gospel, "departure is no longer a spatial category; it can take place *within the cultural space one inhabits.*"[2]

If we want to respond to the call of Abraham—if we, with Volf, believe that departure *is* part and parcel of Christian faith and that, in order to enrich ourselves as disciples, we must broaden our horizons and familiarize ourselves with people, places, and perspectives that are unfamiliar to us—then the best and most proven way to do this is through reading.

"While reading," Maryanne Wolf writes in *Proust and the Squid*, "we can leave our own consciousness and pass over into the consciousness of another person, another age, another culture." We can thus "try on, identify with, and ultimately enter for a brief time the wholly different perspective of another."[3]

This is an oft-touted thing, reading's capacity to help us better understand and develop empathy for another—as well it should be. What often goes unremarked, however, is that reading also helps us develop the capacity to *love*. And while this may seem like an artificial distinction—like a matter of semantic hairsplitting—it is not, for there is all the difference in the world between understanding someone else's perspective and giving oneself over to it. Walking a mile in another's shoes is not the same as sharing one's shoes to make another's journey more comfortable.

Which leads me back to the story.

—

The day after I sent Ankoma the order of worship, I began to notice something quite striking on Facebook. Suddenly, people I had never heard speak out about racial injustice were posting notes in support

of the burgeoning protests. Suddenly, people I had known to be quietly skeptical about the reality of systemic racism were decrying its
evident horrors.

And at first, I was quite heartened by this. But as the day drew
on—and as the day bled into the next—I began to slowly intuit something that both sobered and convicted me. The more I watched these
posts pop up on my Facebook feed and the more I watched folks like
myself advocate for change (and then applaud ourselves for our own
courage), I began to think, *we are hijacking this moment.*

It became suddenly obvious to me that, in our desire to demonstrate that we were on the right side of things—in our desire to
demonstrate that we "understood" the injustice of it all—we were,
despite our sincerity, turning a movement that was ostensibly about
equal rights into a movement that was really about our own moral
righteousness. And like I say, I didn't just behold the problem; instead, I beheld that I was *part* of the problem.

Ankoma and I were scheduled to meet the following day to discuss the order of worship and to further brainstorm logistics of the
event. As I arrived, we made small talk and then began to discuss the
national unrest and the importance of a proper theological response
to it.

Then, finally, Ankoma said, "Well, to the event at hand, then."

"Yes," I said, "but before we go any further, I want to make a confession and offer you an apology." Ankoma looked at me, his brow
furrowed. "It's just," I said, "that in the past forty-eight hours, I have
come to notice that a great many folks seem to be trying to turn this
moment into something different—something more about ourselves
than about a real movement for justice. And I fear that, without meaning to, I have been part of the problem."

"Go on," Ankoma said.

"Well," I said, pointing to my laptop. "This order of worship that
I sent you the other night? I want you to know that I worked really
hard on it; I tried really hard to make it meaningful."

"So, what's the problem?" Ankoma asked.

"The problem," I went on, "is that I now realize that I created a worship service in my own image."

Ankoma sat back and put his fingers to his lips, thinking for a moment. Then he said something that will long stay with me. "You know," he said, "I spent a lot of time this morning praying about how to say that to you—how to tell you that very thing without hurting your feelings—and I appreciate you saying it so that I didn't have to."

From there, we went on to have a valuable and charitable conversation, my confessing to him a sincere desire to be part of the solution and his affirming to me his sincere trust that this was true.

After that, I sat back and let him take the lead, and what ultimately came of it was a deeply moving experience, a community-building event that looked entirely different than the one I had conceived of, an event that was successful for that very reason.

—

"Reading," theologian John Dunne writes, "is a kind of *learning to love*."[4] Maryanne Wolf elaborates: "[Through reading] we welcome the Other as a guest within ourselves, and sometimes we become the Other. For a moment in time, we leave ourselves; and when we return, sometimes expanded and strengthened, we are changed both intellectually and emotionally."[5]

I reference these lines in order to make this crucial point: On the day I realized that I was part of a group unwittingly (and counterproductively) hijacking the cultural moment, I immediately thought of Ralph Ellison's novel *The Invisible Man*. Watching Facebook that day and reading one too many overly curated posts, I suddenly recalled the final sentence of *The Invisible Man* with an arresting exactitude.

But before I share that sentence, I must explain that, a decade earlier, prior to my reading *The Invisible Man*, I spent about eighteen months committedly reading books by African American authors. When I finally got to Ellison's *The Invisible Man*, I came to the book with a sort of moral pride, with a feeling that I was now "one of the good ones," someone in touch with the inequities in the world and someone who, though I could not share the experience of others, at least now understood there was a problem. So was my mentality a problem when I began *The Invisible Man*.

Throughout the novel, Ellison introduces a never-ending parade of do-gooder types, characters who traipse across the pages "helping" in one way or another, through political activism or academic largesse or charitable giving or the like. What I soon began to notice, however, was that while these characters were always performing moral deeds, Ellison, as the author, seemed to be eyeing these characters with suspicion.

And to be perfectly honest, I just didn't get it. Why, I quietly wondered, do these well-intentioned folks continue to warrant such cynicism? But then came the novel's end, and with it, so too came the scales from my eyes. And here, now, is that final sentence: "Being invisible and without substance, a disembodied voice, what else could I do? What else but try to tell you what was really happening *when your eyes were looking through me?*"

———

Volf does not simply stress departure for departure's sake in *Exclusion and Embrace*. Instead, the reason for departure—that is, the reason for leaving one's home "for a land that God will show us"—is to eventually return home *changed and enriched* by the experience.

In other words, Volf is teaching us that when we open ourselves to the ideas and lived experiences of others, we become more fully realized human beings. We become more capable of apprehending the limitations of our own perspectives and of how much wider the world is than we previously imagined. We further recognize our own complicity in the brokenness of things, and we become inspired to repent of it and begin working toward restoration.

Departure, then, is about (momentarily) shuffling off our own sectarian and individual identities so as to more fully embrace the identities and lived experiences of others.

Offering another this sort of "embrace" is an altogether different kind of act than simply trying to "understand" another's experience—as if another's experience were something that could be observed in a laboratory or detailed on a spreadsheet. Which is to say, this willingness to "embrace" is a call to a far deeper and more demanding kind of love than filial love or eros—that is, to a love based on kinship or warm feeling. This kind of love is not about generating emotion; it is about apprehending our responsibility to and for others and about developing sufficient resolve to respond to it.

Embracing another—that is, leaving one's home with the humble hope of being invited into the home of another—is to engage another as a *neighbor*. It is to desire not just to know another but to live in community with him or her; it is to affirm another in a person's particularity without reducing the person to an object of study or superimposing upon him or her one's own image and assumptions.

The point, here, being this: In my experience, reading is the best way to learn how to depart and embrace in this way. It is the best way to *learn how to love*. For not only does reading enable us to learn about another's experience, it allows us (momentarily) to live that experience through another's eyes. When we do this over and over again, with no motivation other than to leave home for a land God will show us, we not only sharpen our understanding and slowly develop our capacity for empathy but soon enough we begin to grow in *love*: and not just in *any* love but in neighborly love—*agapē* love—the kind of love that is less concerned with understanding the other than with embracing the other.

Writes Alan Jacobs: "To recognize the other as a neighbor, in which the other is *purely other* . . . [to be] *outside* what you read but not alienated from it, so that you take up the responsibility of loving that newfound neighbor as yourself—*that* is the philosopher's stone of reading."[6]

This brings us back to *The Invisible Man* and my experience with Ankoma. When I read *The Invisible Man* all those years ago, it was not with the intention of "learning to love," and it was certainly not with the intention of undergoing a life-changing epiphany. Instead, I came to the book with the simple excitement of reading a classic novel—with a certain eagerness to see what the fuss was all about, and, as I said above, with a sort of false pride regarding my preparedness for reading it.

Yet, through reading *The Invisible Man* I apprehended—in a sudden, harrowing moment—how we as human beings are capable of reducing others to objects, capable not just of looking *past* others (which I of course knew) but, in the words of Ellison, of looking *through* others. How we are capable of rendering others *invisible*.

Ellison's novel helped me apprehend how I had confused self-love with true love, and then, a decade later, it helped me understand the kind of departure that would be necessary to embrace the societal moment with the *agapē* it demanded.

As pastors, we are not only responsible for teaching people about Jesus and for ensuring that our members are committed to sound doctrine and social justice; we are also responsible for teaching our members how to *love*—and this is a lesson that can be taught only through the example of our lives.

Thus, as Abraham's progeny and as representatives of God, we must do more than speak syrupy words about love and be able to parse the word's meanings in Greek. So much more than that, we must do the necessary interior work to ensure that people will be able to see in us the markings of "departure" and an evident willingness to "embrace."

Which is to say, our love must be *visible* upon us, lest we continue to go on like clanging cymbals while the rest of the world looks right through us.

Maryanne Wolf asks, "What will happen to . . . readers who never meet and begin to understand the thoughts and feelings of someone totally different? What will happen to readers who begin to lose touch with that feeling of empathy for people outside their ken or kin?"[7] One can imagine Miroslav Volf responding: "They will be increasingly unwilling to follow God into the holy lands God wants to show them."

SECTION TWO

Not Just a Luxury

Reading for Ministry

A FEW YEARS AGO, at a pastors conference in Atlanta, I was having dinner with several seasoned ministers. These were pastors whose names carry a great deal of weight, and it was a joy to hear them reflect on their time in ministry and the friendships they had maintained across the years. I was honored just to be at the table.

About thirty minutes into our dinner, one of the pastors—seated across the table from me—said, "Austin, I've now heard you reference three different books you have recently read. When are you finding time to read these books?"

I was taken aback by the question. This was one of the leading ministers in my network, someone with a PhD and an enormous following, and it was clear to me—simply by the way he framed his question—that he himself had *not* been reading many books.

"Well," I responded to him, "I have lately been *making* time."

He smiled. "Is that time in the office, or time at home?"

I considered his question and then said, "Well, both, actually. I have a program. I read early in the morning; then I carve out time during the workday; and then I read at night after my children are in bed."

The pastor grinned before turning to the other ministers at the table. "Do you guys hear that?" The ministers nodded and chuckled, one even commended me on my "discipline." "I would love to read that much," the pastor then told me. "I just don't have the time." He paused before amending: "No, I suppose that's not true. I *do* have time—but it's at the end of the day, and I'm usually just too worn out by that point. By then I prefer just to watch the news and go to bed: something that doesn't require much active thinking."

I told him that I completely understood. "But you do *like* to read?" I asked him.

He nodded. "Oh, absolutely. I still buy books all the time—you should see the stack I have on my nightstand. I just don't ever have the time to read them. With so much else going on, it just seems like a luxury I can never afford."

As soon as the words left his mouth, I realized that he had just done me an enormous favor: with one short sentence—in fact, with one single *word*—he had just helped me understand why most pastors, including those with a love for reading, seldom take the time to actually do it. Unlike my pastor friend in chapter 2 who fails to read because he doesn't retain most of what he reads, this pastor fails to read because he considers reading a *luxury*. For this pastor, it isn't a question of wanting to read; it is a question of feeling guilty for doing it.

With this one word—"luxury"—I suddenly understood why I had felt such guilt years earlier as I sat reading *The Idiot* in my office. It wasn't just my awareness that there were other ministerial duties I should be performing (though that was absolutely part of it); it was also—and far more significantly—my sense that I was forgoing those duties to *indulge in a luxury*.

And that is the crucial distinction.

There is a big difference between leaving a raft of phone calls unreturned because we are making hospital visits or working on our sermons and failing to return calls because we are, say, getting our daily massage. It is the sense of *luxury* that occasions the guilt.

Therefore, ever since that conversation, I have been endeavoring to convince pastors that we need to reframe our conception of what "time spent reading" actually *is*; we need to stop conceiving of reading as a personal luxury (akin to a daily massage) and begin conceiving of reading as a vocational responsibility.

64

And that is what this second section of the book is about. Having spent time in section 1 demonstrating how reading is in fact more *form*ational than *in*formational, this second section will demonstrate how reading forms us specifically as ministers, sharpening our vocational skills and greatly expanding our pastoral range. As in section 1, this section will take a far more inductive than deductive approach. Here, I will once more do more showing than telling, using further examples from my own ministry to bring to the fore the larger points being made.

Nonetheless, all that has gone before—everything about neuroplasticity, about formation versus information, about virtue shaping and wisdom building, and so on—should be assumed as operative in each of the stories I tell.

In other words, the following chapters will build on section 1 by showing—through illustrations from my own ministry—how a commitment to wide, regular reading forms us not only into more expanded and enriched persons but also—by extension—into more effective preachers, pastoral caregivers, vision-casters, and organizational leaders.

—

6

Reading for Preaching

ONE OF THE FIRST SERMONS I ever preached was a eulogy for my grandfather. I was about one year into seminary, and I had not yet taken a single preaching class. My grandfather, meanwhile, was my hero. It was he who first drew me to Jesus and who first modeled for me a Christ-shaped life; it was he who was my biggest champion when things were up and he who provided me the most thoughtful counsel when things were down. If ever I wanted to get my words exactly right, this eulogy was it. Thus, I labored over my manuscript, writing and rewriting.

As someone who had spent the previous decade working as a writer, I found the sermon-writing process quite different from all writing that had gone before it. It seemed almost like trying to solve a Rubik's Cube, in that I would see the sermon moving in one direction, and then, just as quickly, I would sense that I was building the message around the wrong image, and thus I would shuffle the elements of the sermon, editing and cutting and trying again.

Writing always requires seeing one's way through the process—feeling one's way forward in the dark; writing "by faith and not by sight"—but this was different. My dilemma here wasn't one of form or syntax, or even of direction or purpose; it was instead a problem of clarity—a problem of *ballast*. Given how much I was trying to say, and how little time I had to say it, I needed an image that would pull all these ideas together and enrich each point I was making, all the while stabilizing the sermon and serving as its anchor.

And while I knew this was what I needed, I could not think of a single story or image or anecdote with the proper weightiness to fulfill this purpose. Either it would be too thin to capture the entirety of the message, or it would be so thick as to obfuscate what it was supposed to be enriching.

But then, finally—and all of a sudden—it came to me, and it came with stark clarity. I was reading back over my text, reflecting upon the attributes I was trying to express about my grandfather—his kindness and his gentleness; his goodness and his selflessness; his integrity and his larger-than-life nature—when suddenly, these words bubbled up from a place I did not know I had, a place Fred Craddock refers to as a preacher's "reservoir": "His life was gentle, and the elements so mixed in him that nature might stand up and say to all the world: this was a man."

They are words from Shakespeare's *Julius Caesar*, the final words Mark Antony speaks of Marcus Brutus just before the play ends. And while I had taught this play several times to high school English classes, I had never committed these words to memory nor ever knowingly taken note of them.

Yet here they were, right when I needed them most.

So, I placed the line at the sermon's end, and immediately its effect upon the rest of the sermon was obvious. Like a leitmotif in a composition, this line seamlessly and harmoniously pulled together each individual element of the sermon.

⁓

In his book *Reading for Preaching*, Cornelius Plantinga Jr. writes: "The reading preacher will discover that great writers know the road to the human heart and, once at their destination, know how to move our hearts. To the preacher, knowing what stirs human hearts is golden and not at all because heart stirring is a good project all by itself. No, the preacher wants his heart stirred because he will then have some idea how the power and beauty of the gospel might be presented so that the heart of his brothers and sisters may also be moved."[1]

Plantinga's book gives wonderful articulation to what I, as a preacher, have in the time since that day experienced on account of my commitment to reading. By plumbing the depths of human experience—by walking in another's shoes and by wrestling with complicated situations—a reading preacher gets an increasingly stronger sense of what will move a congregation, and also—and more importantly—a stronger sense of *why* it will move them.

And it is the "why" that Plantinga is drawing our attention to in the above quotation. Plantinga is reminding us that as pastors we are not entertainers or performers; we are not stand-up comedians or TED talk presenters. Instead, we are emissaries of Jesus Christ, called by God to present the good news of salvation to all who will listen.

Thus, the mark of a good sermon is not whether it brings tears to members' eyes or brings the house down with laughter (though those things can be praiseworthy and desirable); it is instead whether the tears and the laughter enable one *to more clearly see himself or herself in the unfolding story of God's love for the world.*

And that, Plantinga's book persuades, is what wide reading helps us as preachers do for our listeners. Through our exposure to so many new experiences and phenomena, and through our immersion in so much new knowledge and information, we begin to more fully understand why language about, say, loneliness affects hearers the way it does, or why stories about sacrifice reach us at the deep registers they do. Then, knowing these things, we are able to anticipate how a certain poetic phrase, or a certain heartwarming anecdote, or a certain piece of data will move or disarm or surprise our hearers, *all in service of opening each hearer's heart to the good news of the gospel.*

In Plantinga's book, he highlights the myriad effects reading can have on sermon preparation: how immersing ourselves in the words of the masters will inevitably rub off on our own craft; how reading supplies us with useful quotes and imagery to use in our own writing; how reading helps us close the experiential distance between ourselves and others; how reading enriches our understanding of major Christian themes such as sin, redemption, and grace. Plantinga compellingly covers all this and more, and I highly commend his book to you.

These are all skills that develop at the "subterranean level" that James K. A. Smith writes about in *Imagining the Kingdom*, and thus they cannot be developed in a strictly utilitarian fashion. Meaning, if we read a book with an eye toward how we can immediately use a quote or an image from it in our next sermon, the quote or image we use will almost always sound dissonant or forced. Likewise, if we read a book with the intention of capturing a writer's style so as to channel it in our own writing, our voice will inevitably sound fraudulent and affected.

Instead, as preachers we *read by faith*, trusting that while we don't yet see how our reading will be useful in our sermon prep and delivery, we nonetheless know that it *will* be, because with each successive book and article and essay we read, our filters are being enriched and our reservoirs are being filled, our understanding of human nature is being expanded and our wisdom is being increased.

Thus, we trust that we are slowly being turned from what Walter Brueggemann might call "purveyors of prose" into "preachers of poetry." Brueggemann writes: "The task and possibility of preaching is to open out the good news of the gospel with alternative modes of speech—speech that is dramatic, artistic . . . [that] assaults imagination and pushes out the presumed world in which most of us are trapped . . . *a poetic occasion* that moves powerfully to expose *the prose reductions around us* as false."[2]

In other words, for Brueggemann our everyday language as human beings is typically surface level and stale; our daily lived experience, flat and mundane. But the poetic preacher, should he or she have the temerity and the skill to do so, has the awesome opportunity to enliven language so as to deepen and enrich one's lived experience.

For Brueggemann, this "poetic" voice is not about using flowery or ornate language; it's instead about knowing how to use our speech with intentionality, touching carefully upon those items that "stir the heart," always in service of expanding a sense of what's possible.

Taken together, then, Plantinga's *Reading for Preaching* and Brueggemann's *Finally Comes the Poet* bring to the fore the point I am trying to make in this chapter, which is that a steady commitment to reading shapes the vessel of preachers and fills the reservoir from which they have to pull, thereby enabling them to disrupt the felt-flatness of their listeners' everyday realities by speaking words that will help them imagine new possibilities.

Moreover, I am claiming that such a capacity develops only in qualitative, noninstrumental ways. To wit: a lovely quote from T. S. Eliot won't penetrate a listener's heart just because it's a lovely quote or just because it's by T. S. Eliot; instead, for the quote to penetrate— for it to broaden and transform a hearer in the way Brueggemann is describing—it has to be precisely the right quote (at precisely the right time) to bring out the "flavor" of everything else the sermon is saying. And either a preacher "has" that quote when he or she needs it (and has the proper instincts to know where to place it) or a preacher doesn't; the preacher can't just go out "looking for it."

In the same way, a powerful image from, say, *To the Lighthouse* will not open a listener to new possibilities for her life simply because she appreciates a good story or happens to admire Virginia Woolf; instead, the image must *breathe life* into the dry bones of what has gone before (in the sermon) and what will come right after.

And the only way for us as preachers to have access to such "fitting" quotes and such "life-breathing" images is to read long enough, and widely enough, and committedly enough to have a reservoir that, even when we don't realize it, is all the while collecting these things, a reservoir from which they will emerge when we need them most.

Which brings me back to the story of writing my grandfather's eulogy. What I experienced that day—the perfect quote (at the perfect time) emerging from a reservoir I didn't know I had—has happened to me hundreds, if not thousands, of times since.

And for that reason, I never start a sermon with a quote or image or allusion or reference in mind; instead, I start with the gospel point I intend to convey, and then, without actively soliciting it, like a match struck in the darkness, a phrase will suddenly occur, or an image will come to mind, and it will be precisely the quote or the image I need to pull the sermon together and, as Plantinga says, pull also the heartstrings of those who will be listening.

Case in point: when I finished delivering my grandfather's eulogy that long-ago afternoon and our family lingered in the aftermath to receive condolences, one of the men in attendance—someone who had long admired my grandfather and looked up to him as a sort of mentor—approached me and asked me for a copy of my manuscript, saying that while he had always appreciated my grandfather, he had never before made the mental connection between his admiration for him and the gentleness of my grandfather's character. He told me that in hearing it put this way, he knew that it was true, and that this had convicted him about his own sense of harshness toward others, and that it had caused him to want to be a gentler person himself.

In other words, the eulogy had opened him and expanded him, penetrating the flatness of his lived experience and nudging him toward a new possibility.

"That Shakespeare quote," he said to me, "that said it all. Would you mind sharing it with me?"

It was a poetic moment in a prose-filled world, and I knew right then that, yes, I'd be trying to share it with him—and with others like him—for the rest of my life.

Reading for Pastoral Care

I SAID EARLIER THAT, in my opinion, Eugene Peterson is the pastor-reader par excellence. I don't make such a claim lightly. Having read most of Peterson's books, and having found his spirit to ring true time and time again, I am convinced that Peterson was not only a pastor who practiced what he preached but also a pastor who practiced what he read.

Which is to say that Peterson, more than any pastor I'm aware of, regularly extolled the virtues of reading. Pick up any Peterson title, and not only are you sure to find numerous literary references in the work but you are just as likely to find Peterson digressing in order to explain how vital he believes reading to be for a pastor.

Peterson's various insights into the vocational benefits of reading are nowhere more compelling than in the places where he writes about pastoral caregiving. In *Run with the Horses*, one of Peterson's earliest books, he writes, "Lives cannot be read as newspaper reports on current events; they are unabridged novels with character and plot development, each paragraph essential for mature appreciation."[1]

I have long been struck by his words "mature appreciation." It's as if Peterson is saying that, as pastors, to interpret human beings on the basis of the words they are *currently* speaking, or the problems they are *currently* presenting, is not only to provide an attenuated sort of pastoral care but also to telegraph a certain form of immaturity, one rooted in a fear of complexity and a need to offer quick resolutions—much as it would be to read about a lavish party at Jay Gatsby's house and, knowing nothing of Gatsby's humble origins, hastily conclude that he throws such parties simply to put on airs. It would be to completely miss the point. "The *before*," Peterson writes, "is the root system of the visible *now*."

For years I held onto that insight, and then, like a divine gift, I came upon Peterson's *Subversive Spirituality*, where he elaborates on what this "mature appreciation" looks like in practice. "The first book on pastoral care that ever meant anything to me personally or vocationally," Peterson writes, "is *Ulysses*, James Joyce's novel."[2] Prior to reading *Ulysses*, Peterson had never found pastoral care to be a particularly "creative" aspect of his ministerial vocation. "I knew that it was important and I accepted that it had to be carried out, whether I felt like it or not, but . . . it was not very interesting."

Reading *Ulysses*, however, changed all that. Peterson writes that about six hundred pages into the novel, he woke up to the genius of what Joyce was up to. Here was a thousand-page book detailing a single day in the altogether ordinary life of an altogether ordinary man—yet somehow these seemingly mundane details continued to build atop one another until suddenly Peterson realized that this ordinary man, Leopold Bloom, was everyone: that each of us is Leopold Bloom, and that Leopold Bloom is each person we encounter.

It was the care and attention Joyce gave to each aspect of Bloom's life that moved Peterson so deeply, the way each detail took on greater meaning in light of the narrative that had gone before it. "*This* is the pastor's work," Peterson explains, "to look at each person in [one's] parish with the same imagination, insight, and comprehensiveness with which Joyce looked at Leopold Bloom."

After this epiphany, each pastoral visit became for Peterson not only an encounter with a person but an immersion in a living novel, each conversation offering him a unique and compelling and *still-unfolding* story. "I [now] find myself," he writes, "listening for nuances, making connections, remembering, anticipating, watching how the verbs work, watching for signs of atonement, reconciliation, and sanctification. I am sitting before these people as Joyce sat before his typewriter, watching a story come into existence."

Reading these words was pivotal for me, and not only because I love James Joyce. Rather, these words helped me tease out the implications of what Peterson had hinted at long before in *Run with the Horses*; for here, Peterson was not only explaining, but was in fact showing, how to handle a person's story with "mature appreciation."

"I no longer consider these times duties of pastoral care," Peterson concludes, "but rather, occasions for original research on the stories being shaped in [people's] lives by the living Christ—stories in which I sometimes get to put a sentence."

—

Several years ago, I was afforded the opportunity to "put a sentence" at the end of a ninety-four-year-old church member's story. The man was an eastern Kentucky firebrand, a Will Campbell–style preacher who loved Jesus of Nazareth, the downtrodden of eastern Kentucky, and the national Democratic Party—in which order, I was never quite sure.

His name was Bob Lockhart, and by the time I arrived in Kentucky he was ninety years old. He was equal parts Baptist preacher and stand-up comedian. The first time I met him he tried out all his best material on me, the most memorable line being about how his wife called him "Bob" when she was mad at him but "Robert" when she wanted to make love. Bob was legendary in eastern Kentucky for being the man who, when offering a prayer at a standing-room-only event for the sitting governor, prayed for "those peckerwoods" on the local county school board.

So, that was Bob.

But here, too, was another thing about Bob: Bob loved to learn. In fact, Bob couldn't get enough of learning. Having grown up at a time and in a place where farm children like himself were not often provided the opportunity to have an education, Bob made it a point to defy the odds and become an intellectual. So much so that, when I first went to visit Bob at his house, I found him sitting in his den with his eyes closed, listening (because his vision was now failing him) to a Great Courses lecture on tape. It was a lecture on biophysics.

In the nearly four years I went to visit Bob, I almost always found him listening to a Great Course such as this. During those visits, Bob shared with me a great many things. He was an expert storyteller, and to this day countless of his stories stay with me. But while each of his stories was compelling, there were three in particular that, in light of everything else Bob told me over the years, seemed pivotal to me—that is, seemed to be stories that, like key passages in a novel, were central to understanding Bob's larger story.

The first was about growing up on the farm in eastern Kentucky during the Great Depression, defying the odds not only to finish high school but then to go on to college and seminary. Bob would recount the way that local, more privileged boys taunted him for the school he'd gone to, and it was clear to me as Bob told this story that he still, in a very certain way, saw himself as that young farm boy, still needing to prove himself to a world that might consider him unworthy.

Then there was the story of the young crippled man in the town to which Bob was first called to minister. This young man had been something of a town pariah, not only on account of his physical deformity but also on account of the porn store he ran on the outskirts of town. Bob told me the man had come to him one day at the church, had broken down and bared his soul, and Bob could see the obvious hurt and trauma that society had wrought on the man. Therefore, Bob took the man in, inviting him for dinners at his own home and dining with him at local restaurants.

This soon landed Bob crosswise with certain self-righteous members of his own church. Eventually, Bob baptized the young man in a local river, because the church wouldn't allow the man to be formally baptized in the church's baptistry. "He was pitiful," Bob said. "And those people were awful to him. Treated him like a damn dog. Like he was less than human."

Telling me this, Bob looked off. "That boy died soon after I baptized him. Got drunk and somehow drowned himself in the river. I preached his funeral a few days later, and hardly a person was there."

Bob then got silent, as if embarrassed about growing emotional. Then, with tears in his eyes, he said to me (as if to explain himself): "I don't care what you know about theology; if you don't have compassion as a pastor, you ain't got nothin'."

Now, *that* was a memorable story.

Finally, there is the story of how, midway through his ministry, Bob traded in his pastorate in order to work in the local juvenile delinquency program because he was burdened by how many poverty-born young adults in eastern Kentucky were becoming trapped in the legal system, teenagers who, Bob said, "never had a damn shot to begin with."

For two decades, Bob worked to help young adults such as these find their way out of legal trouble, many of them going on to get degrees and to work in fields such as law, medicine, and the ministry. Once Bob showed me a letter from one of these former delinquents—now a doctor practicing medicine just outside of Washington, DC—thanking Bob for all that he had done for him. Then, after finally retiring from this work, Bob went back into the ministry for another twenty years.

This was just who Bob was.

So it was that, one afternoon in the late spring, I received a call letting me know that Bob was in the hospital. He had been fighting cancer since I'd known him, and recently the cancer had begun to spread rapidly. I showed up to visit him, and when I arrived I found his daughter, Bobbie, sitting beside him as he slept.

"Oh, he'll want to see you, Austin," she said to me, standing to give me a hug. "Let me wake him up. But I'll warn you, he hasn't been very talkative. His words aren't very clear and he gets quickly exhausted."

Bobbie then woke Bob up, whispering, "Daddy, the preacher's here." Bob struggled to come to, and it was evident that he was confused and disoriented. When his eyes registered who I was, though, he shifted his body as if to regain a sense of control and decorum.

I greeted him and told him how glad I was to see him, and I assured him that everyone at the church was praying for him. He nodded, and then, turning to Bobbie, he whispered something. Bobbie leaned in closer to hear what he was saying, and then she said, "Oh, yes. Austin, he wants you to see what he's been listening to since he's been in here."

She then pulled from her purse a plastic case and handed it over to me. It was yet another Great Course, this one called "Voltaire and the Triumph of the Enlightenment."

I looked at the title and then I looked to Bob, who was eagerly studying me to see my response. By this point, I had been immersed in Bob's story for nearly four years, all the while taking care to interpret his story with "mature appreciation," always eager to see how new plot developments would shed light on various details I'd heard before. Now, in this moment, aware that his story was drawing to an end, I suddenly apprehended—in not just an intellectual but in an *experiential* way—what Eugene Peterson meant about "listening for nuances, making connections, remembering . . . watching for signs of atonement, reconciliation, and sanctification."

For here was this ninety-four-year-old man who had beaten the odds—this giant of a man whose influence on the world had been titanic—who, now on his deathbed, still felt compelled to impress his young pastor by proving how interested he was in the French Enlightenment.

As Peterson would say, the connections in Bob's story were suddenly clear to me, as was the key to atonement, reconciliation, and sanctification. Thus, I took the opportunity to "put a sentence"—one that, like the final sentence of *The Great Gatsby*,[3] was intended to draw together all that had gone before, clarifying Bob's life story and underscoring its central theme.

And so, clasping Bob's hand, I said, "I don't care what you know about Voltaire; but I do know this: if you don't have compassion as a pastor, you ain't got nothin'."

Bob, comprehending both the intent and the significance of these words, squeezed my hand and then shut his eyes.

And those were the final words I ever spoke to Bob Lockhart.

—

"The self maintains its sense of being a self primarily by means of the interpretation of life as a story," writes Charles V. Gerkin in *The Living Human Document*. "Each of us has a story."[4]

Bob's story is an example of the point I hope to make clear in this chapter, which is that if we attend to each pastoral visit as an encounter with a "living human document," prepared to "interpret" each story with "mature appreciation," we will become more insightful and more capable caregivers.

A central thesis of Gerkin's book is that, while people often know the *details* of their own lives, they do not necessarily see the larger story those details are embedded in. Thus, by attending to people's words as if we are "reading a human document," quietly making inferences and drawing connections, pastoral caregivers can help people see their lives as *stories*, thereby providing a deeper sense of clarity and significance to their lived experience.

To be able to do this, however, requires (as Peterson says) "more than just showing up." In other words, we can't just assume that because we suddenly view the individuals before us as living human documents, we are therefore going to be wise interpreters. Instead, to become wise interpreters, we must first develop such interpretive skills through the reading of *non*human documents: books, novels, journals, essays, and so on. Only then can the skills from our reading begin to shape our skills for caregiving.

As Neal Plantinga writes in *Reading for Preaching,* "Identification with others may be partly instinctive, but it is also partly deliberate— *and thus dependent upon an educated attempt to stretch our sympathies across circumstantial distance."*[5]

Seldom are the connections in one's story as clear and as prominent as they were for me in Bob's. However, if we commit ourselves to more frequent reading; to making educated attempts to stretch ourselves across circumstantial distances; to applying our interpretive skills to the human documents before us; and to attending to these human documents with mature appreciation, the larger story being told throughout these documents *will* eventually emerge, the connections between "the now" and "the before" coming more clearly into focus as the current gets borne back ceaselessly into the past.

8

Reading for Vision Casting

THE WINTER RELIEF MINISTRY at the church I served in Kentucky came into being through months of reading—and then required a great deal of prayer, discernment, and discussion.

Technically, I suppose, it began when Paul Sims pointed out to our missions committee that the calendar was nearing winter and a great number of homeless persons in eastern Kentucky were going to be left without shelter from the cold. The area lacked a sufficient homeless shelter, and an increasingly large population of homeless persons was living in the woods and under bridges nearby.

"Then we should provide them shelter," one of our committee members said. "Simple as that."

Well, not really.

The problem—at least, the *first* problem—was that we didn't have anywhere to *do* such a thing. Our facilities simply could not function as a homeless shelter.

"Well, in that case, we can work out a deal with a local hotel," another member said. "Isn't there one that the church already works with?" Paul and I nodded. "Great, then let's see if they'll work with us on this," the committee member said.

Long story short (and momentarily skipping over some very important backstory), we did, and the hotel said yes. Our missions committee worked out a plan for the church to open its Family Life Center each evening at five, at which time folks could check in, receive a warm meal, and then be driven by vans to the local hotel.

And to our great delight, the plan worked. Not only did our ministry receive a stunning amount of regional (and even national) press in its first weeks, but the entire community began to partner with us to serve meals and financially support the new ministry.

However, not everyone in our church felt comfortable about what we were doing. And with each passing day, the ministry was drawing more and more homeless and impoverished people to our campus. Which soon led a kind woman named Emma, a member of the church for decades, to voice her reservations.

"I just think we are enabling these people," Emma said to me, as we sat together in my office. "They don't work; they just sit around all day at the library—many of them doing drugs—and they just wait there for us to open the doors and feed them and give them somewhere to sleep. And I just don't see how this is a *ministry*."

Looking back, the timing of this conversation with Emma was providential. For I had recently finished reading James K. A. Smith's *Imagining the Kingdom*, and had been struck by a particular concept in the book: "the sanctification of perception."[1] By this, Smith is referring to the recalibration of our imaginations, the removal of various prejudices and preoccupations that, like scales upon our eyes, occlude a kingdom vision.

Thus, when Emma said, "I just don't *see* how this is a ministry," I couldn't help but recall Smith. Of course she couldn't see it, I realized; she, like all of us, had to first undergo a sanctification of perception.

Had Emma come to me prior to my having read that book, I likely would have spent an hour trying to explain to her what a "holistic eschatology" was. I probably would have rattled on about N. T. Wright and Jürgen Moltmann and Tim Keller and Walter Rauschenbusch. Instead, I still had these words from Smith fresh in mind: "If hearts are going to be aimed toward God's Kingdom, they'll be won over by good storytellers . . . [because] sanctifying perception requires restor(y)ing the imagination."

Therefore, rather than try to convince Emma of how offering food and warm beds to those in need *did* constitute a viable ministry, I shared two books with her, both of which several members of our church had been reading together over the past several months: Matthew Desmond's *Evicted*, which is about the difficulty of finding and maintaining housing when living below the poverty line, and Beth Macy's *Dopesick*, which is about the opioid epidemic and the way it is ravaging the country, particularly in areas like rural Appalachia.

"I tell you what," I said, assuring Emma that I understood and appreciated her concern. "How about you read these, and then let's meet again in two weeks to talk more about it."

Emma assured me that she would read them, then we prayed together and she left.

—

As I said, the reason I gave Emma *these* particular books is that several people in our church had already been reading them together. Which is to say, long before Paul had brought up the impending winter and the absence of a local homeless shelter, several of us had already been reading about, and growing concerned about, the homeless in our community.

Meanwhile, in the missions committee meeting I described above, thirty minutes after we agreed to approach the local hotel about partnering with us, someone on the committee, while granting the significance of the problem and the importance of a viable solution, suddenly asked, "But is this really the business of the church?"

Paul asked the man what he meant.

"I mean, important as something like this would be," the man responded, "is feeding and housing people really a *church ministry*? I mean, just giving them food and shelter—and that's it? How is this actually going to save any souls?"

I remember the question like it was yesterday. And looking back, I believe the question to have been a pivotal moment in the ongoing story of our church's winter relief ministry. Not just because it was a valid question and because we needed a satisfactory answer to it in order to receive the votes necessary to move forward, but because what this man was asking was the same question that we would be asked many more times throughout the years.

Perhaps because I had been reading James K. A. Smith at the time, or perhaps because *The Brothers Karamazov* is one of my favorite novels, it occurred to me that the best response to this question was not theological but imaginative; that the question was best answered not through discursion but through storytelling.

"There's a scene in *The Brothers Karamazov*," I suddenly began, "where an elderly priest is approached by a woman in the community who is worried about her faith. This woman tells the priest that she often dreams about serving her church, about doing impressive things in the name of her faith—about 'saving souls,' if you will. But then, after she considers how little her efforts will actually *change* things, and after she considers how long her hours of service will be and how little evidence of transformation they will ultimately yield, she never acts on these ideas, and instead just leaves them as lovely daydreams in her mind."

The members of the committee all chuckled (they were used at this point to my literary digressions).

"*So*," one of them said, "what's the point?"

"*So*," I said, "the priest then responds to the woman by saying this: 'Love in dreams is greedy for immediate action, rapidly performed and in the sight of all. But active love is labor and fortitude.'"

After a moment of silence, one of the committee members said, "That's a great story, Austin. But what does that have to do with our winter relief ministry?"

"It has everything to do with it," I responded. "Don't you see? If we *don't* do this, we will be just like that woman. Think about it. Right now we share a common dream about how we might actually make a difference in this community. I mean, do you realize how amazing that alone is? That we share a common dream and a common vision? Yet, like that woman, we fear that our service alone won't be enough, that we need to see instantaneous transformations in order to make our service and our investment feel worthwhile." I paused. "And that is why Dostoyevsky's words are so important: 'Love in dreams *is* greedy for immediate action—but active love is labor and fortitude.'

"If we do this," I went on, "souls *will* be saved and lives *will* be transformed, but it won't happen on our timetable or in the ways we anticipate it—it will instead happen when and how God determines best. We just have to commit to active love and fortitude. And trust God for the rest."

Looking back, I don't know how convincing I was, but fortunately no one put up a counterargument, and we soon voted to move forward.

The key takeaway from this part of the story is that the time many of us spent reading together proved to be critical in helping our church form this vision, and drawing connections between ourselves and a character from classic literature proved particularly helpful in imagining our way forward.

—

Please don't think that any of this happened overnight, and that the applications of what we'd read to our vision for this ministry operated like a sudden epiphany. Instead, the vision settled in and took time. Certain of us read those books—and others like them—over the course of many months, not in a weekend. And as much as I'd like to pretend that my *Brothers Karamazov* speech had had the effect of Knute Rockne's "Win One for the Gipper," it was not nearly that climactic.

That said, the books *were* indispensable in helping us cast our vision—first in forming it, later in conceiving of how to implement it, and finally in convincing others to get involved.

Which leads me back to Emma. Around that same time, I had preached a sermon in which I'd referenced Flannery O'Connor's short story "Revelation," and, unbeknownst to me, the sermon had stuck with Emma. Thus, when Emma came back to visit me a few weeks later, and when I asked her if she had read the books, she told me that she had but that she'd first like to talk with me about that sermon.

"Okay," I told her. "What would you like to talk about?"

"The end of it," Emma said. "I didn't really understand it—yet it's stuck with me ever since."

"Any chance you could remind me what I said?" I smiled.

Emma laughed. "It wasn't the end of your sermon, but the end of the story you referenced. You said something about the woman in the story having 'her virtues burned off,' and something about the poor and the dirty from her town marching up to heaven singing hallelujah."

"Ah," I said. "Yes. It's a famous image. The woman, Mrs. Turpin, has all her life felt like God is in her debt due to her commitment to manners and rectitude, yet she is blissfully unaware of how eaten alive she is by arrogance and her own feelings of superiority. She looks down on all of those beneath her in her community, particularly the poor and the destitute. But then she has this encounter where she believes God has spoken to her—and, most surprisingly, spoken to her through someone she considers beneath her, someone she deems sloppy and worthless. And this 'revelation' rattles her to her core, leading up to that final line you're talking about, where it's evening and she is alone on her farm, and suddenly she sees a vision of the saints marching upward to heaven, the poor and the mannerless leading the way, the people of culture and decorum like herself bringing up the rear."

I then stood up and walked to my bookshelf. "Here," I said. "I'll read that final line for you." Pulling down my copy of *The Complete Stories*, I flipped to the proper page. "In the woods around her the invisible cricket choruses had struck up," I read, "but what she heard

86

were the voices of the souls climbing upward into the starry field and shouting hallelujah."

"That's it." Emma nodded. "That's the line. And I haven't been able to get it out of my mind."

I let the moment hang in silence. "Do you have any thoughts as to why that may be?" I finally asked.

Emma looked troubled. "No, I really don't," she said. "But it's stuck with me, and it's bothered me ever since." I let the room sit in silence. "Well," she said, growing uncomfortable and changing the topic, "I *did* read them." As she said this, she handed back my copies of *Evicted* and *Dopesick*.

"And?"

Emma laughed. "And this won't surprise you, but I found *them* troubling, too."

"Oh my," I said.

Emma laughed again. "'Oh my,' is right. But don't take offense at that. I'm glad I read them. I really am. I just need time to digest them a little more." I told her that I completely understood. Then she said to me, "I've been thinking about it, and I think I'd like to come help at the ministry tomorrow night. See what it's all about."

I told her that we would love to have her join us. Emma then thanked me and asked to pray with me, letting me know that she needed to be on her way.

———

"The church in the power of the spirit is not yet the Kingdom of God," Jürgen Moltmann writes in *The Church in the Power of the Spirit*, "but is its anticipation in history . . . in provisional finality the church witnesses to the kingdom of God as the goal of history *in the midst of history*. In this sense the church of Jesus Christ is the people of the kingdom of God."[2]

Moltmann's work played a huge role in the formation of our winter relief ministry—if not so much directly as imaginatively—and it just so happened that I was thinking of Moltmann when I watched Emma come through the door the following night and make her way to the kitchen.

It had been an especially cold day, which meant that it was an incredibly busy night at our ministry. Despite the clamor and the chaos, though, Emma went straight to the kitchen, found an apron, asked for directions, and plugged right into the daily doings of the ministry.

Throughout the evening, as I went from table to table, checking on our guests and listening to their stories, I continually saw Emma coming in and out of the kitchen, running plates and refilling drinks. She was engaged and committed. Later that night, after several van loads had already departed for the hotel, I noticed Emma, her apron still on, standing just outside the kitchen and staring across the room at one of the tables.

I followed Emma's gaze and saw five of our "usuals" sitting and laughing with three of our regular volunteers. By now, our "usuals" and our "regular volunteers" not only knew one another by name but had become quite friendly with one another, having shared by this point many meals and stories together.

And as I watched Emma study this table, taking in the tableau of a circuit court judge, the chief medical officer of the hospital, a sitting city council member, a known prostitute, a lesbian couple, a twenty-one-year-old car thief, and a thrice-convicted felon all sitting together laughing, their joy palpable, I saw something happen to Emma. Not only did I see her virtues being burned away, but I saw her soul being saved.

Here before her was active love, in all its labor and fortitude. And moreover, here before her were the fruits that such active love was bearing: not only the idealized transformation of the people who were being served but the slow transformation of the people doing the serving.

In short, here was the church in the power of the spirit, anticipating the kingdom of God in the midst of history.

Standing there beside that kitchen, studying that table, I saw the sanctification of Emma's perception beginning to take place. And as she listened to the roar of that table's laughter, I knew she was hearing the sound of their souls climbing upward, all of them shouting hallelujah.

9

Reading for Leadership

When I wrote earlier about a pastor involved in the church growth movement who reads books by Michael Hyatt and Carey Nieuwhof, noted Christian authors who write about leadership, I certainly didn't mean to make light of such books (I own several of them myself). I simply wanted to highlight how, as pastors, we need to remember that we are far more than "leaders."

In this chapter, however, I want to make clear that we are also nothing less, either.

Leadership—by which I mean the capacity to inspire, organize, manage, and sustain a group—is a central aspect of a pastor's vocation. And this extends to several different *types* of groups: one's staff, one's committees, one's membership, one's wider community, and many other groups, besides.

I have read many leadership books over the years, books like *The 7 Habits of Highly Effective People* and *The Organized Executive* and *Leading Change* and *How to Win Friends and Influence People*. I have likewise read many specifically Christian leadership books from folks like John Maxwell and Andy Stanley, along with the aforementioned Michael Hyatt.

Several of these books have proven helpful, but I have consistently found Hyatt to be the most compelling of these leadership authors—

and not so much because of the particular skills I have gleaned from his books but because Hyatt so regularly extols the benefits of reading for leadership.

"If you want to lead," Hyatt writes, "you simply must read. It's one of the surest ways to develop the qualities that will make you stand out and simultaneously equip you to lead as your influence grows." Hyatt elaborates: "Reading has the potential to help us boost our emotional IQ and better identify with people. And empathy is a vital leadership skill for creating alignment, understanding motivation, setting organizational goals, and more."[1] No less a leadership authority than Warren Buffett agrees with Hyatt, claiming, "I read and I think. And because I do, I make fewer impulsive decisions than others."[2]

Hyatt's and Buffett's words track with testimonies of numerous other high-profile leader-readers, people such as Bill Gates, Elon Musk, and former president Barack Obama. Each of these leaders regularly lifts up reading as a leadership virtue, not simply on account of the informational value one acquires through reading but on account of the broadening effect such reading inspires. (Note how in the quote above, Buffett says his reading makes him more patient and more self-controlled, not more knowledgeable and more informed.)

All of this is to say: there are countless books on leadership techniques and on developing leadership identity, and I certainly encourage pastors to take time to read such books.

For the purposes of *this* book, however, I want to key in on what leader-readers like Hyatt and Buffett say about the intangible ways that reading benefits leaders. And to do that, I am going to tell two stories that took place in 2020 at the height of the COVID-19 pandemic.

―

By the time autumn of that year arrived, my church had grown increasingly frustrated by the global shutdowns and sequestrations necessitated by COVID-19. In-person worship and in-person activities had been suspended for over eight months, and things such as closings, masking requirements, and social distancing were becoming increasingly politicized, compounding the complexities for church leadership.

Meanwhile, our church council, the decision-making body for our COVID-19 policies, had been receiving frequent phone calls and lengthy emails telling us what we should or should not be doing as we moved forward. And while these arguments used different language and ostensibly sought to make different points, they could essentially be distilled into variations of the following:

1. We are all free and responsible adults; therefore, we need to open back up and give each adult the opportunity to decide whether or not to assume the risk involved with coming.

2. It is unfortunate that this virus affects certain people more adversely than it does others; and it is certainly lamentable that some may in fact die from it. However, because only a small fraction of the population will be so direly affected by it—and because the vast majority of us will experience it like a flu or a common cold—we therefore need to get back on with church business as usual.

3. Concern for the wider community is far more important than concern for any one individual, so one's personal desire to engage with church friends or to receive personal edification must take a backseat to concern for the common good. Therefore, we should not even consider reopening church at this point.

It was an agonizing time to be a pastor, as many readers will no doubt recall. We pastors were not responsible for the anxiety caused by the pandemic, nor were we trained epidemiologists with novel insights into microbiology and virus mutation. That didn't mean, though, that people didn't expect us to somehow come up with a solution that could please everyone and simultaneously prevent our churches from tearing apart.

I was deeply torn because I found all three arguments to be persuasive. I *did* think that personal responsibility mattered and that honoring individual choice was important. I *did* think that most people would ultimately be okay were we to come back, and that only a fraction would be adversely affected. And I *did* think that the common good mattered and that considerations of the whole were at least as important as considerations of the individual, if not more so.

Thus, I felt emotionally and intellectually torn, constantly being pulled in different and contradictory directions depending on whom I'd spoken with last, each argument seeming both logical and compelling.

Then, lying in bed one night, asking myself how I had suddenly become so changeable—how such contradictory arguments could all obtain such purchase with me—the answer occurred to me in a flash: "Every one of the arguments is logically valid," my inner ear heard the philosopher Alasdair MacIntyre whispering. "The conclusions *do* follow from the premises. But the rival premises are such that we possess no rational way of weighing the claims of one against another."[3]

It was a key argument from MacIntyre's landmark book *After Virtue*, and, as it came to me, I immediately realized that *this* was the core problem: the reason I had become so changeable and persuadable was because each argument *was* logical and persuasive on its own terms—I was simply failing to recognize "the conceptual incommensurability of the rival arguments."

—

Around this time I happened to mention to our music minister, James Bennett, that I had just reread *Gilead*. I told James how influential *Gilead* had been in my decision to become a pastor, and then I joked about how dubious that decision had proven to be, seeing as the COVID-19 pandemic—along with several other deeply fraught situations currently taking place at the church—was wearing me thin.

"Perhaps I *shouldn't* have read *Gilead*," I joked to James. "Because right about now I'm increasingly uncertain that I know what I am doing."

After that conversation, unbeknownst to me, James purchased a copy of *Gilead*. James is a classically trained music minister who, like Paul Sims before him, is not only in the twilight of a long and storied career but, also like Paul Sims, quickly became not only a cherished mentor but also one of my dearest friends, someone closer to me than family. So it was that my spirits were greatly lifted a few days later when I received the following texts from James, the first one quoting this line from *Gilead*: "I'm writing this in part to tell you that if you ever wonder what you've done in your life, and everyone does wonder sooner or later, you have been God's grace to me, a miracle, something more than a miracle." That message was then followed by this one: "I read this and thought of you, of course."

After this sweet note, which greatly bolstered my confidence, I texted James back and asked if he was enjoying the book. James, who is among the most literate and sharp-eyed readers/editors I know, wrote back: "I'm LOVING it!"

This led to regular conversations between James and me about *Gilead*—about parts James was liking; about ways we could both relate to certain characters; about how we'd both been moved by certain passages. This went on for several days until one day, upon referencing the novel during a staff meeting, we told our other staff minister, Lucy Cauthen, about how James was reading *Gilead* and about how much he was loving it.

"Have you read it?" I asked Lucy.

Lucy shook her head. "No, I never have," she said.

"Oh, Lucy, you *have* to," James responded. "It's wonderful."

And suddenly, as the words left James's mouth, an idea occurred to me, one that years later I am deeply grateful for, because it led to one of the most moving and formational group-bonding experiences I have ever had. "You know," I said to them. "Not only are there three novels in the *Gilead* saga—but Robinson's fourth novel, *Jack*, is supposed to be released in a few weeks. What if we were to read all four of them together and then meet at James's lake house to discuss them?"

To my great delight, the suggestion was enthusiastically received, and an hour later, as our meeting ended, James and Lucy left my office to go procure copies of *Gilead*, *Home*, and *Lila*, the three published books in the *Gilead* saga.

⁓

Two months later, with the COVID-19 crisis continuing to rage on in the world around us, we met on the back porch of James's lake house, our marked-up and dog-eared copies of Marilynne Robinson's novels before us.

By this time, we were exhausted as a pastoral team. Beyond the enormous amount of energy that it had taken to simply "do" church throughout those interminable COVID-19 weeks, we were also worn down by the competing pressures that were constantly being placed upon us. We were overworked and feeling underappreciated.

Each of us had read all four novels in a matter of two months, meaning that, by the time we met to discuss them, we had not only been living together in that lovely world created by Marilynne Robinson but we had been immersed in it. Therefore, as we sat talking that day, and as we spoke of Jack Boughton and Lila Ames and Della Miles, we talked about them like they were old friends of ours.

Moreover, we talked about them for hours. And the longer we sat talking, the clearer it became to each of us that not only had we enjoyed these stories, but that by reading them together—by living together in this fictional world and by coming together to talk about these characters and their lives—we were together sharing something special, something far bigger than the sum total of the novels' plotlines.

In other words, we realized that something was happening to *us* on account of it.

This all came home for us when we zeroed in on *Home*, the second novel in the series and the one that James and Lucy ultimately liked the most. (For the record, *Gilead* will always remain my personal favorite.) As we reflected on the characters in *Home*, and on the magnetic pull that a yearning for "home" has on human beings, and on how each of us at the table had, in our own way, undergone the same loss of "home" that sits at the emotional center of this exquisite novel, we began to realize what had formed between us over the past year.

The three of us had been called to this church within months of one another, each of us having uprooted our lives—having left "home," so to speak—to come serve in this new place with these new people. Then, months later, a global crisis was dropped in our laps, on top of which we were still performing daily triage in response to major traumas the church had undergone in its recent past.

And we'd been through it together. All of it. And consequently, we had become our own little family. We loved one another. We supported one another. We believed in one another. We trusted one another.

Looking back, I suppose we already knew those things, but there was something about sitting around that table and discussing "trust" and "commitment" and "family" and "heartbreak" through the lens of these novels that made us more aware of what we had become. Of *who* we had become.

At a certain point in the conversation, responding to a comment I had made about the worn-down minister Robert Boughton, James said, "Maybe he was just tired."

"We're all 'just tired,'" I said, trusting they understood my implication.

To which Lucy, always hip to the emotional undercurrents taking place around her, turned to a page from *Home* and read the following line: "Weary or bitter or bewildered as we may be, God is faithful. He lets us wander so we will know what it means to come home."

Which leads me back to my first story. As I lay in bed that night with Alasdair MacIntyre's insight from *After Virtue* in mind, I suddenly realized that this insight held the key to my entire dilemma.

Each of the rival arguments seemed persuasive to me, I realized, because each one *was* logically conclusive. The problem was that once placed in opposition to the others, there was no neutral ground for adjudicating between them. They had, as MacIntyre describes it, "incommensurable conceptualities."

The following morning I reread the first two chapters of *After Virtue*. Then, being fully persuaded that this was indeed the problem, I pulled Michael Sandel's *Justice* from my shelf, along with MacIntyre's *Whose Justice, Which Rationality*, Francis Fukuyama's *Identity*, and Robert Putnam's *Bowling Alone*.

It is unnecessary for us to get into the weeds about how and why each of these books was beneficial to me in the moment; what matters is how I came by them and how I knew to pull them down from my shelf. All these books were texts I had read of my own volition sometime *after* seminary. And this is a crucial point, because far too often we, as pastors, neglect to continue to read challenging works of theology, philosophy, sociology, and science once we have finished our formal education.

Significantly, until this moment, I had never had cause (at least not to my awareness) to "use" any of these books since reading them. Yet now, years later, a moment had come when they were suddenly indispensable. I simply would not have been able to unlock my sense of inner conflict or anguish had I never read these particular books.

After reading key passages from these texts (and after rereading *Justice* in its entirety), I sat down at my laptop and created a presentation for our church council that would demonstrate how all the arguments could be understood in light of three overarching moral frameworks, and how each one was rooted in a rival—and "incommensurable"—moral vision.

The first, I showed them, was rooted in a moral libertarian frame-work, the emphasis being on personal freedom; the second, in a utilitarian framework, the emphasis being on the greatest good for the greatest number; and the third, in a collectivist framework, the emphasis being on the general will and the common good. Finally, I showed them what a kingdom of God framework looks like in con-tradistinction to the other three, after which I led a discussion of what the biblical vision of shalom looks like in contrast to the highest goods set forth by these other moral visions.

It was a hit. Not only was the presentation well received but it eased a great deal of tension among members of the council. We came to a decision we all felt good about, and we ended the meeting knowing that even if some people in the church would be rendered unhappy by our decision, we had solid reasons to justify and defend the decision we'd come to.

The following morning, as James, Lucy, and I met in my office and debriefed on the meeting the night before, James expressed gratitude and relief that we had together made it through yet one more fraught situation. As I looked to James and then to Lucy, and as I saw in their faces love for and trust in me, I saw in them both the unmistakable sign of God's faithfulness, and I knew then and there what it meant to come home.

FOR WHATEVER REASON

How to Become a Pastor-Reader

B Y THIS POINT, you are no doubt wondering when and how you can find the time to do the kind of reading that this book has been recommending. Perhaps, like the minister friends I mentioned in the introduction, you have caught a glimpse of how reading could be beneficial for your ministry, and perhaps you even feel persuaded to give such reading a try.

If so, the question you now face is: *When?*

As I have noted several times, our schedules as ministers are notoriously full. Each day brings all-new, unanticipated challenges—hospitalizations, sudden deaths, premature births, unexpected (and sometimes outrageous) phone calls and emails—on top of the items already filling our calendars. So, *when,* it is fair to ask, could a pastor possibly find time to do the kind of reading for which this book has been advocating?

The answer to that question lies in the distinction between reading as a luxury and reading as a vocational responsibility. If we perceive reading to be a luxury, then, yes, finding time for reading in our already-busy schedules is nearly impossible. Just ask the highly regarded minister from section 2 with the ever-growing stack of books beside his bed.

However, if we perceive reading to be a vocational responsibility, then all sorts of possibilities open up for us. For just as we find time to fit in pastoral visits each day—even if our schedules are already stretched thin—so too can we begin to squeeze in hours for reading.

That, then, is where section 3 will begin: by encouraging us to think of time spent reading *as* a pastoral visit. From there, we will discuss how to turn reading into a spiritual discipline; how to approach reading with a proper spirit; how to choose what to read; how to collect and file reading for later use; and finally, how to approach biblical reading with the same wonder and curiosity as we approach all other reading.

If the first two sections of this book have effectively been addressing the questions, *"What* is a pastor-reader?" and *"Why* be a pastor-reader?" this last section will be addressing the much more practical question, *"How* can one be a pastor-reader?"

If you have been at all inspired or persuaded thus far, then the following pages will help you further envision how you might begin to implement this kind of reading program into your own daily routine and ministry.

—

10

Reading as a Pastoral Visit

I WELL REMEMBER my first official pastoral visit. It was to the home of a man named Harold Adkins.

I had been living in Kentucky for about five days at the time, having preached my first sermon and having taught my first Bible study, and Paul Sims recommended that I begin visiting certain of our homebound members. Paul suggested that I visit Harold first because, at eighty-nine, Paul suspected Harold wouldn't be around much longer.

"It will be helpful for you to get to know folks like Harold so you'll be prepared to do their funerals," Paul told me.

I agreed with Paul. When I arrived at Harold's place for our visit, I was well prepared to dazzle him with the rich insights I'd just gleaned from Paul Tillich's *Perspectives on 19th and 20th Century Protestant Theology*, a book I'd found at a used bookstore just prior to moving to Kentucky. I was also, of course, prepared to discuss other theologians. And if it turned out that Harold wanted to discuss philosophy, well, that was also fine, because I had just finished reading Baylor professor Stephen Evans's *Faith beyond Reason*, and it would be my pleasure to talk with Harold about that.

In other words, I arrived at Harold's house that day thinking that this was what I had been waiting for. That this was what I had become a *pastor* for. All my years of theological education were finally about to be put to use. Finally, I would be answering people's big questions, helping them sort through their deepest theological quandaries.

So, imagine my surprise when upon my arrival Harold wanted to talk to me about ballroom dancing.

"Ballroom dancing?"

"Yes," Harold said. "I did it for many years. Only stopped a few years ago."

"Oh yeah?" I asked, busily trying to think of a creative way to redirect the conversation.

"Yes," Harold responded. "It was a real joy of mine."

"So how did you get into it?" I asked him, aware that I needed to at least momentarily indulge the topic.

Harold shifted in his seat, thinking for a moment. Finally, he said, "My wife got me into doing it."

"Yeah?" I asked.

Harold laughed. "Yeah. Originally, I didn't want to have anything to do with it. I had my own interests—not to mention my own work—keeping me plenty busy, and ballroom dancing just didn't appeal to me."

"So how did she change your mind?" I asked.

Harold then looked at me the way a father looks at a son when he is about to impart hard-won wisdom. "I finally realized it didn't *matter* that I didn't want to do it—because what mattered was that *she* wanted to do it, and that if I wanted to be a decent husband, I ought to start thinking about someone other than myself."

Though Harold could not have known it at the time, his words affected me greatly. Because at that very moment, my own wife, April, had been quietly signaling to me that she needed more attention than I had lately been giving her.

April and I had just uprooted our lives and, with an eighteen-month-old in tow, had moved to a completely foreign place. Meanwhile, April was due to give birth to our second child (under the care of doctors she didn't know) in six weeks, and she had just gone from working full time to temporarily staying at home. She felt lonely and disoriented, and she wanted me to spend more time with her in the evenings, talking and watching television.

It wasn't that I didn't want to talk or watch television with her—it was simply that, in my mind, I needed to be reading things like Paul Tillich's *Perspectives on 19th and 20th Century Protestant Theology* and Stephen Evans's *Faith beyond Reason*. Things that would help me answer the burning questions I was so certain my new members were going to be asking me.

In other words, without realizing it, I'd been putting her off. And I'd been doing this, I suddenly realized, because, in Harold's words, "I had my own interests—not to mention my own work"—and because talking and watching television "just didn't seem appealing to me."

Whenever Niccolò Machiavelli was about to read a book by a classic writer, he would change into his finest clothing. He believed such authors deserved a reader's highest respect. To Machiavelli's mind, these were not just long-dead progenitors of clever ideas; these were instead living presences, their voices speaking across the ages as if they were seated at the table right before him.

And not only did Machiavelli dress up for these writers, he also spoke back to them. "I am not ashamed to speak with them," he writes, "and to ask them the reasons for their actions; and they in their kindness answer me."[1]

While I would never put forward Machiavelli as a virtuous philosopher—and while I, myself, have never donned a tie and sport coat just to read someone like Leo Tolstoy—I nonetheless think his reason for getting dressed up to read is a helpful reminder about what the reading act really *is*. For, far more than a passive encounter with words on a page, the reading act is a two-way conversation between two living beings—even if one of those living beings has been dead for millennia.

What the Machiavelli illustration so aptly highlights is how we, as readers, are not just passive recipients in these conversations. Instead, we come to the conversation with our own perspectives and personalities, attending carefully and respectfully to the author's voice and all the while "speaking back" in response. In this way, by the time the conversation has finished, we have inevitably been shaped and affected by the reading exchange.

Consider this example from my own reading of Tolstoy's *Anna Karenina*, a novel I read soon after moving to Kentucky and visiting with Harold Adkins. Flipping through my copy of the novel, I find the following margin note beside a passage about the unwillingness of the protagonist, Levin, to commit to a serious relationship: "Levin needs to put his romantic idealism behind him."

But then, eighty pages later, next to a marginal note that says, "Am I Levin?" I find *this* passage underlined: "Though he had thought that he had the most precise notions of family life, he had, like all men, involuntarily pictured it to himself only as the enjoyment of love, which nothing should hinder and from which nothing should detract. He was supposed, as he understood it, to do his work and to rest from it in the happiness of love."

Then, finally, a few pages after that, this passage is underlined and starred: "He [Levin] understood not only that she was close to him, but that he no longer knew where she ended and he began." And scrawled beside *that* passage is a note that simply says, "April."

The point being: At one point in my engagement with the text, I clearly thought that I had something to teach Tolstoy (and if not Tolstoy, then at least his fictional character Levin). Then, some pages later, I realized that perhaps Tolstoy had more to teach me than I'd thought. Then, finally, I realized that perhaps Tolstoy had something to teach me about *myself*.

In other words, here in the margin notes of my copy of *Anna Karenina* we can find documentation of a give-and-take between

Tolstoy and me, the recorded evidence of a conversation he and I shared many years ago.

—

What does this have to do with finding time to read?

Here's what. In a vocation that keeps a pastor going a hundred miles a minute, a vocation in which carving out an extra hour or two per day on one's calendar *just to read* seems impossible, the best way to do it is to begin conceiving of reading as a regular pastoral duty. And the best way to do that is to begin conceiving of reading as a pastoral visit—which, at its most fundamental level, reading *is*.

Which leads me back to my visit with Harold Adkins. When I showed up to visit with Harold that day, I showed up the same way that many people show up to the reading act: which is to say, I showed up with the assumption that this would be a one-way mode of communication. Now, I obviously knew that Harold would be *talking* during our visit, but I naïvely assumed that I would be the one offering pearls of wisdom while Harold would be the one passively benefiting from my scholarly erudition.

Instead, though, for whatever benefit I may have been to Harold that day, Harold was of far greater benefit to me. I left Harold's house suddenly aware of the extent to which I had been neglecting the person who mattered most to me, the one who, as Levin puts it, is so close to me that I no longer know where she starts and I end. What I learned as a pastoral caregiver from that experience was a fundamental lesson, which is that pastoral visits are *always* two-way conversations, each participant—both pastor and parishioner—being all the while shaped and affected by the exchange.

And the point here is that the reading act is likewise a two-way conversation, one wherein both participants—both reader and author—are all the while being shaped and affected by the exchange. As Alan Jacobs puts it, "Reading is supposed to be about the encounter with other minds, not an opportunity to return to the endlessly appealing subject of Me."[2]

Certainly, Tolstoy didn't change his mind because of my active participation with his novel, but through the mental and emotional act of processing Tolstoy's ideas and engaging with his characters, I was all the while *speaking back* to the great master. Which means it was a conversation. And just like my conversation with Harold, I was changed and enriched by this conversation with Tolstoy, further wizened and prepared by it for future pastoral visits.

Such, then, is the benefit of conceiving of one's time spent reading as a pastoral visit: our literary dialogue partners inevitably prepare us for the flesh-and-blood dialogue partners with whom we will soon be conversing.

I only got to visit with Harold once more before he died, and I was far more prepared for the conversation on that visit than I had been the time before. When Harold once more brought up ballroom dancing, I said to him, "It's not really the dancing part that you miss about ballroom dancing, is it?"

Harold paused, and then reflectively said, "No. It's not." He was silent for several seconds, and then he said, "She's been gone for nearly eight years now. And I miss her every day."

Harold had kept dancing well into his eighties, I now realized, not because he loved dancing but because he loved his wife. And even though she had been gone for some time, he no longer knew where she ended and he began. Ballroom dancing was just a way to feel still connected to her.

After sitting quietly, Harold then said, "I just wish I'd had more time to dance with her. That I'd been more attentive and started sooner." He paused once more. "I hope you can understand what I mean by that."

"Yes," I gently responded. "I can."

—

Endorsing this approach to reading as pastoral visit, Eugene Peterson writes in *The Contemplative Pastor*, "I venture to prescribe appointments with myself to take care of the needs not only of my body, but also of my mind and emotions, my spirit and imagination. One week, in addition to daily half-hour conferences with St. Paul, my calendar reserved a two-hour block of time with Fyodor Dostoevsky."[3]

The key here, according to Peterson, is blocking off the time; setting the daily appointment; getting the "meeting" on the calendar. "The appointment calendar," Peterson explains, "is the one thing everyone in our society accepts without cavil as authoritative.... When I appeal to my appointment calendar, I am beyond criticism."

So takeaway number 1 for how to become a pastor-reader is this: conceive of reading as a pastoral visit, and begin scheduling at least one hour for it each day.

Whether or not Machiavelli blocked off such calendar time for conversations with folks like Plato, we cannot be certain. But we *can* be certain that if we block out calendar time of our own, then pastoral visits with folks like Tolstoy will inevitably make us better caregivers to folks like Harold Adkins.

Because whether we get dressed up in our Sunday finest for such visits or not, we'll be increasingly more prepared to discuss things like ballroom dancing and marital commitment.

11

Reading as a Spiritual Discipline

A FEW YEARS ago I was having coffee with a minister friend who had recently become a pastor-reader. This friend had listened to me ramble long enough about my own love for reading—and about my conviction that reading makes a minister a more effective practitioner—and he had decided that he wanted to give it a try, too.

Therefore, I had encouraged him to schedule an hour per day to "meet" with various novelists and nonfiction writers, treating these daily meetings as pastoral visits. He had now been dutifully doing this for about two months, and this coffee meeting was our first opportunity to discuss.

"So, how's it going?" I asked him.

"Well, I'm not sure," he responded. "I've read some stuff that I like, but I'm not sure whether it's helping me yet."

"Just stay the course," I assured him. "Soon enough, it will."

He paused. "Yeah, well. That's the thing. I mean, I don't doubt that it does for you. In fact, I've *seen* it work for you—I've watched you pull some random literary reference into a conversation and seen how it adds clarity to what you're saying. So, I know it works for *you*."

"So, what's the problem?" I asked him.

"The problem," he responded, "is that I just don't see how one hour per day in my office is going to get me there. I mean, I'm barely into my fourth book at this pace—and I've been reading *short* books."

"Go on," I said.

He scratched his beard. "Austin, you told me ten minutes ago that you just finished reading *Moby Dick*."

"Yeah, so?"

"So, I know *Moby Dick*. It's like eight hundred pages. Eight hundred *dense* pages. And unless you are averaging about five 'pastoral visits' per day, there is no possible way you have been doing all of that reading in your office."

I laughed. "No, you're right. I haven't been meeting with Herman Melville for five hours per day at my office. Most of that was done at home."

He looked at me with a frown. "So, you're reading at home, too?"

"Yeah," I responded. "Sure, I am."

"But you only mentioned reading for an hour in the office," he said, "and treating that hour like a pastoral visit. You didn't say anything about reading at home, too."

I sat forward, suddenly aware of a gaping hole in the way that I had been presenting my theory about becoming a pastor-reader. Looking at my friend's bemused face, I realized that I had become so insistent on encouraging pastors to read during the workday that I had failed to mention that carving out time to read at home was important, too.

My friend was absolutely right: there is no way one can finish a book like *Moby Dick* through one-hour sittings in one's office (at least not in any reasonable amount of time). "I am so sorry," I said to my friend. "Yes, I find that reading at home is very important, too."

Dejectedly, my friend looked down into his coffee.

—

It had been an oversight on my part, but I'd later come to find that this oversight was actually the thing that made my friend's transformation into a pastor-reader possible. Because research shows that in order to form a new habit—which always requires unlearning (or de-forming) other, older habits—one is best served by focusing on developing one new "pattern." That is, on adding one new practice to one's daily routine.

This one new practice is what neuroscientists call a "keystone" habit, because it's the bedrock behavioral change that enables all subsequent changes to take place. Research has found that if we overload our neurological system with several big changes at once, adding several new practices all at the same time, our system will reject the attempted changes because habit formation is never a matter of willpower alone. The spirit may be willing, but the neural networks are weak.[1]

Or, more precisely: the spirit may be willing, but the neural networks are *rigid*. If, for example, we are fast-food junkies who suddenly decide we want to lose weight and therefore cut all unhealthy foods cold turkey, our systems will reject our grand attempt, not only making us physically ill but also, in the process, ensuring that we run right back to McDonald's to make ourselves feel better. But if we begin by changing just *one* unhealthy thing per day—say, cutting out soft drinks, or eating a salad for lunch—and then slowly keep building on this "keystone" habit, over time healthier eating will truly become a habit.

In this same way, forming a reading habit also requires beginning with a "keystone" habit, adding just enough of a reading commitment to one's day, but not too much.

Had my friend, who had not been reading at all until he began carving out time for these "pastoral visits," begun by reading an hour in his office and *also* an hour in the morning, he likely would have never made it. Like the fast-food junkie running back to McDonald's, he likely would have put the book back on the shelf and begun refilling his calendar with other pastoral responsibilities.

Thus, even though I had done it unintentionally, it turns out that instructing him to read only an hour per day in his office proved to be the very thing that enabled him to form the habit. Now, several years later, this friend reads approximately two hours per day—one hour at home and one hour in the office—and this habit would likely have never taken hold had he started by trying to read two hours each day.

—

Having said that, I want to encourage us to stop using the word "habit" when we talk about our reading as pastor-readers and begin using the word "discipline." In fact, from here on, I want us to begin conceiving of our reading habit as a "spiritual discipline."

As we will soon see, this is precisely what a reading habit can and should become: a spiritual discipline. In his landmark book *Celebration of Discipline*, Richard J. Foster reminds us how important "disciplines" are for a spiritual life. A much-resisted word in contemporary culture, "disciplines" refers to the constraints that counterintuitively lead us to personal and spiritual liberation. Disciplining ourselves to pray regularly and disciplining ourselves to quietly and unassumingly perform daily acts of service—*committing ourselves to such mundane routines*—slowly become second nature to us, shaping us from the inside out and the outside in.[2]

In the same way, reading can become a spiritual discipline for us if we will slowly allow it to become a routine function of our daily lives.

Henri Nouwen, writing about the cultivation of spiritual disciplines, encourages seekers to do three things: (1) set aside *a definite time*, (2) set aside *a special place*, and (3) set aside *a single focus*.[3] In my own experience, Nouwen's method is very effective for cultivating the spiritual discipline of reading.

Take *Moby Dick*, for example. My pastor friend was right; I didn't read that book in my office. Where I did read it, though, was just as important as my *having* read it. Because if I hadn't had a special place for my reading—along with a definite time for reading it and a single focus while doing it—I would never have been able to finish such a long and demanding book.

I read *Moby Dick* for two uninterrupted hours each morning in a yellow chair by a corner window in the living room of our home in Corbin, Kentucky, while the rest of my household slept. Looking back on that house and on those countless hours I spent reading there, I can now see with clear hindsight just how important that *place* was for my reading. And I don't mean by that the *specifics* of the place; I mean the simple fact of *being* in that place each day as I read.

In *The Stone Reader*, a documentary that is essentially a bibliophile's account of forming his own reading habit, the filmmaker Mark Moskowitz says of reading, "The place becomes a book." He means the place where one reads a book gets intertwined in one's brain with one's memories of that book.

In my experience, Moskowitz is right. When I think back all these years later to certain scenes from *Moby Dick*, my memories of the novel are inextricably connected with my memories of that yellow chair, and of that corner window, and of that morning stretch from 4:45 to 6:45 when I would sit quietly reading, and of the hot coffee that would sit just beside me as I read. And it's not only *Moby Dick* that is attached in my memory to that place, but so many other books as well.

To my pastor friend's point, I never would have been able to finish those books by reading one hour per day in my office. Instead, finishing so many large and challenging books required me to set aside a definite time and a special place for reading at home, too.

Moreover, as Nouwen claims, it also required of me a special focus, an ability to block out all other distractions to focus exclusively on the book before me. Fortunately, when one conceives of reading as a spiritual discipline, this kind of focus quickly becomes second nature. For, as Foster writes, "The mind will always take on an order conforming to that upon which it concentrates."

That has been my own experience with reading.

If we will just show up to the special place at the definite time, the book will not only become the place, it will quickly become the single focus.

—

When my friend and I were finishing coffee that day, I encouraged him to begin carving out another hour each day for reading.

"When do *you* do it?" he asked me.

"I wake up each morning at 4:45," I told him, "and then I read until 6:45, which is when Ada and Julianna get up for school. At that point, I stop to make them breakfast and help April pack their lunches for school."

"Man," he replied. "I don't know that I can do two hours each morning. Particularly on top of the hour I am already doing in the office."

I shook my head. "You don't have to. In fact, the hour you're already doing is enough on its own. You're going to see the benefits from it, I'm certain of it." I paused. "But in order to *maximize* the benefits, and more importantly, in order to be further enriched by the process, I *do* think it will be beneficial to add an extra thirty minutes to an hour to what you're already doing."

"Then why do you do *two* more hours each morning?" he asked.

"Because I love it," I said. "It's my passion. And because it works for me and for my family's current rhythms. But others might only want to do—or might only be *able* to do—one or two hours, which is totally fine, and is also totally enough." I reflected for a moment and then went on. "You know, there's no set formula for how to do this—the only thing necessary is to actually *do* it. To actually read. To actually cultivate it as a discipline."

"What do you mean by 'cultivate it as a discipline'?" he asked.

"I mean pick a special place to read, and set a definite time each day to do it, and while you do it, focus all of your attention on what you're reading." He watched me, as if expecting me to go on. "Now,

I *do* think you need *at least* an hour," I finished, "but you certainly don't have to read three hours a day in order to have your life enriched and your ministry strengthened."

"So, one hour in the morning and one hour in my office," he repeated to me.

"Yes," I said. "Try that, and then let's meet again to discuss in a couple of months."

"I'll give it a shot," he told me, and then we went our separate ways.

———

At its most basic level, a spiritual discipline is a repeated practice that nourishes one's soul and expands one's sense of the grandeur of God and the connectedness of creation. And while many people falsely assume that a spiritual discipline, by definition, involves either abstaining from something or letting something go, most spiritual leaders also extol the soul-nourishing benefits of picking something up and engaging something new.

For instance, Dallas Willard, in *The Spirit of the Disciplines*, explains that all disciplines of abstinence ought to be counterbalanced and supplemented by disciplines of engagement.[4] For Willard, as for Foster and Nouwen, these disciplines of engagement include things like prayer and study and confession and communal fellowship. One discipline of engagement that these writers spend little to no time talking about, however, is the discipline of general reading—that is, the "study" of books other than the Bible or other related theological texts.

I believe this is a big oversight.

For while Bible study and the reading of theological texts are no doubt soul nourishing, so too are novels and short stories and biographies and works of nonfiction that broaden our knowledge of the world, deepen our insight into the human condition, and expand our appreciation for creation's complexity.

Just because a book does not formally mention "God" does not mean that God is not to be found right smack in the middle of the story. And just because a novel does not formally cite Scripture does not mean there are not lessons to be gleaned about what it means to love our neighbors and be our brothers' and sisters' keepers.

Such fundamental theological topics—these ideas of "ultimate concern"—often lurk just beneath the surface of the written page, as deep and profound and mysterious as the watery depths that call out to Ishmael and that keep Ahab obsessing over that inscrutable white whale. "There is one knows not what sweet mystery about this sea, whose gently awful stirrings seem to speak of some hidden soul beneath." That is Melville's Ishmael speaking about the ocean, but it could well have been Richard Foster or Henri Nouwen or Dallas Willard speaking about the edifying nature of general reading, if only they'd extended their range of spiritual disciplines to include non-theological texts. For there is almost always a sweet mystery about the books one reads, a mystery that temporarily binds the hidden soul of the writer to the hidden soul of the reader.

Such, I'd soon find out, had become the case for my friend. When we met a few months later for coffee, he told me that he had successfully added an extra hour of reading to his daily schedule and that he had experienced his first "connection" between the sermon he was working on and something he had earlier read in his daily reading program. Also, an elderly woman he was visiting in the hospital said something that reminded him of a passage from a novel he'd recently read, which gave him insight into how more deftly to extend care to her.

"It works," he said to me.

"Yes," I said in response. "It does."

"But you can never control it," he said. "That's the crazy part. It just comes to you . . . unbidden."

I thought about that for a moment. "Yes," I said, deciding that I liked his word very much. "That's precisely how it works. It comes to us *unbidden*. It comes to us as *one unknown*, you might say."

"That's Schweitzer, right?"

Laughing, I responded, "Now you sound like a pastor-reader."

"Though each habit means relatively little on its own," writes Charles Duhigg in *The Power of Habit*, "over time . . . the way we organize our thoughts and work routines have enormous impacts on our health, productivity, and happiness."[5]

In the same way, so too does each hour spent reading—on its own—mean "relatively little." However, if done over and over again, consistently and committedly, those combined hours eventually come to exert an enormous impact on us. And not just on our health, productivity, and happiness, but also on our spiritual well-being and on our effectiveness as pastoral leaders.

So takeaway number 2 for how to become a pastor-reader is this: don't start by trying to read too much at once. It will never work. Instead, start with forty-five minutes to an hour—preferably in your office—and try to keep that up for two months. Meanwhile, don't think about what you're beginning as a "habit" that you're trying to form; instead, think of it as a spiritual discipline, something you are "picking up" in order to attend to God and nourish your soul. Then, finally, set aside a definite time and a special place to do your daily reading, and make sure to maintain a single focus while doing it.

If you do, there is no telling what sweet mysteries you will eventually find, what gentle stirrings of the hidden soul you will hear emanating from beneath.

Do I sound crazy saying that?

If so, just call me Ishmael.

Reading with a Proper Spirit

JUST THE OTHER DAY I was browsing my bookshelves, looking for my copy of Faulkner's *The Unvanquished* for a sermon I was writing, when I came upon the spine of Owen Flanagan's *The Problem of the Soul*, a philosophical treatment on the mind-body dualism dilemma. It had been years since I'd read the book—in fact, I'd forgotten I *had* read it (much less owned it)—so, out of curiosity, I pulled the book from my shelf and began leafing through it.

On page 11, I came across the following underlined passage: "We are language users and words and signs have meaning. But evolution does not require that meaning be born of meaning or that meaning be produced by a Meaner. The Mother of All Meaning—whatever that may mean—did not possess meaning or act from a wellspring or reservoir of meaning."[1]

To my great dismay, I found this margin note just beside that passage: "*Ridiculous!*"

Looking back on the young man who made such a curt and dismissive margin note (on page 11, no less!), I see a reader who was given to approaching certain books with his arms—and mind—tightly closed, a reader who came to certain authors with deep suspiciousness and a lack of charity. I see a reader who demonstrates little to no humility whatsoever.

In the same way, when I open my copy of Dallas Willard's *The Divine Conspiracy*, a book I bought years ago from Amazon and which arrived with copious markings and margin notes, I find the following note from the previous owner on page 391: "I don't think Christians who believe in the Eternal Personality have any idea of what they are wishing on themselves!" And then this, two pages later: "This is such a stretch!" And then finally this, three pages after that: "Incomprehensible literalism!"

Now, chances are—based on what I can glean from the many margin notes throughout the book—the previous owner of my copy of *The Divine Conspiracy* would not have found Flanagan's take on the origin of meaning to be nearly so "ridiculous" as I did, just as I, unlike this previous owner, take all of Dallas Willard's words quite seriously. In other words, had the previous owner and I traded books, the margin notes in these two copies would likely have a far rosier and more positive spirit about them.

But what Jesus says of loving others goes for loving authors as well: If you love only those whom you find it easy to love, what credit is that to you?

In short, both I and the former owner of my copy of *The Divine Conspiracy* were guilty of something a pastor-reader ought never to be guilty of: approaching the reading act with a lack of humility, charity, and hospitality.

—

Neal Plantinga refers to the disposition with which pastor-readers must come to our reading as "receptivity." Plantinga and I were once talking about the formative power of reading, about how wide, curious reading has the capacity to form human beings into evermore virtuous people, when Plantinga stopped midsentence and added an important caveat to our shared thesis. "Reading is no doubt imperative for the pastor," Plantinga said, "but so too is a spirit of receptivity to the text he or she is reading. Without the proper spirit, reading will not occasion the kind of moral and spiritual formation we are talking about."

Plantinga's point is well taken. No matter how much—or how widely—one reads, if one is not reading with a charitable eye toward the author, along with a curious disposition toward the material one is reading, one will not be formed in the meritorious ways this book is suggesting. A particularly sobering reminder of this fact comes from George Steiner, who cautions us "that one can read Goethe or Rilke in the evening, that he can play Bach and Schubert, and go to his work at Auschwitz the next day."

Thus, everything we have thus far said in this book now warrants an arresting caveat: *Lest we approach our reading with a disposition of humility, hospitality, and receptivity, our reading will not of its own accord form us into the ever-expanding, morally sharpened human beings we seek to become.*

For that, we must first be charitable readers.

—

Recently, I was listening to a podcast conversation between Miroslav Volf and Krista Tippet, host of NPR's *On Being*, and I was struck by the way Volf characterized Tippet's program.[2] "It seems to me that what you are doing is curating conversations on the art of being human," Volf said.

Delighted by that characterization, Tippet explained how she prepared for interviews: "What I'm really interested in are the animating questions behind the human enterprise . . . and *if I define my curiosity that way*, then I have to be listening and looking at such a range of how humanity manifests in lives and disciplines and pursuits."

When Tippet said the words "if I define my curiosity that way," my ears perked up, because it occurred to me that the way Tippet was describing her approach to interviewing subjects on her radio program was the same way that I describe the pastoral approach to daily reading. As pastor-readers, we too need to "define the curiosity" that causes us to read as "an interest in the animating questions behind the human enterprise."

Meanwhile, as I listened to Volf and Tippet go deeper into their conversation, I began to realize that Tippet, in her responses to Volf, was perfectly articulating the "spirit of receptivity" that Neal Plantinga had years earlier talked to me about. Thus, when Volf asked Tippet, "How do you take yourself into the space where your interlocutors are?" and Tippet responded with the following, I felt as if she were reading my mind: "I approach [it] as an act of hospitality. . . . My primary intention is to be fascinated by particularity, and go deep into that."

—

No one has written more directly and more compellingly about approaching the reading act with a humble and charitable spirit than has Alan Jacobs. In his *A Theology of Reading: The Hermeneutics of Love*, Jacobs makes a sustained case for why the disposition with which one comes to the reading act makes all the difference. If one does not begin with a spirit of humility, Jacobs argues, accepting *as a gift* the book itself as well as the effort that went into writing it, then already one has greatly limited the capacity of the book to teach and inspire. "No one can practice hermeneutical charity who is unwilling to receive a poem, a story—a work—as a gift," Jacobs writes.[3]

Looking back, I most certainly did not accept Owen Flanagan's *The Problem of the Soul* as a gift. In fact, to the best of my memory, I read *The Problem of the Soul* back to back to back with Edward O. Wilson's *On Human Nature* and Thomas Nagel's *Mind and Cosmos*, each of which I read in response to Francis Fukuyama's *Our Posthuman Future* and Steven Pinker's *The Blank Slate: The Modern Denial of Human Nature*.

In short, it was a period in which I was fascinated by the philosophical conversation surrounding what human nature *is*, and what the human soul *is*, and I was marshaling credentialed academics to agree with my already-formed position ("There *is* such a thing as human nature," "There *is* such a thing as a human soul") and then, satisfied, reading credentialed academics who held alternative viewpoints from mine—*just to say I had read both sides.*

Now, I think this warrants our momentarily pausing to consider just how breathtakingly arrogant and obtuse this was.

On the basis of having read two accounts (*two!*) that accorded with my own view of things, I then read three other accounts *just to say I'd read them*—and *then* had the hubris to act as if, in reading them, I had somehow intellectually stood toe-to-toe with three of the most esteemed scholars alive.

In *The Pleasures of Reading in an Age of Distraction*, Jacobs cites the eighteenth-century scientist G. C. Lichtenberg as writing, "A book is like a mirror: if an ass looks in, you can't expect an apostle to look out."[4] Lichtenberg was right. Because when I open my copy of Flanagan's book all these years later and consider my own margin notes, I certainly don't find an apostle looking back at me.

———

Now, the fact that it was *this* book in which I found such a dismissive margin note only underscores the point I am trying to make in this chapter, which is that everything rises and falls on the degree of humility and charitableness that a reader brings to his or her reading.

I say this on account of something I witnessed Owen Flanagan, the author of the book, do many years later. My friend (and former professor) Christian Miller, a highly regarded philosopher who is an orthodox Christian, posted on Facebook a few years ago that he had just published an entry called "Empirical Approaches to Moral Character" in the highly reputed *Stanford Encyclopedia of Philosophy*. Under the Facebook post, I saw the following comment: "Congrats! Well done!" The note was from none other than renowned Duke philosophy professor Owen Flanagan.

The point being: Owen Flanagan well knows that he and Christian Miller hold very different views on questions of ultimate concern such as theism and human nature, yet Flanagan nonetheless showed Miller a great deal more godliness and humanity than I had showed Flanagan when reading his *Problem of the Soul.*

To Jacobs's point, Flanagan seemed to accept Miller's article as a gift, whether or not he agreed with what Miller actually said. Flanagan seemed to understand far better than I did (when I read his book) that questions about the human enterprise were animating what Miller had written, and therefore that whatever Miller said in the piece was to be approached with hospitality, that his own intention as a reader was to be fascinated with particularity and to desire to go deep into it.

In other words, Flanagan seemed to understand that Miller—like all of us who write and try to express ourselves—was ultimately trying to curate a conversation on the art of being human.

Now, granted, I am only speculating here because, outside of this one Facebook comment, I know nothing else about Owen Flanagan—but that's the point of this whole chapter. Perhaps I'd know a lot more about Flanagan had I simply heeded Neal Plantinga's advice and approached Flanagan's book with a proper spirit of receptivity.

⁓

In *Didascalicon*, a book written by the twelfth-century monk Hugh of Saint Victor, aspiring pastor-readers can find the following advice: "For the reader there are three lessons taught by humility that are particularly important. First, that he hold no knowledge or writing whatsoever in contempt. Second, that he not blush to learn from any man. Third, that when he has attained learning himself, he not look down upon anyone else."[5]

So, takeaway number 3 for how to become a pastor-reader is this: no matter the topic and no matter the author, hold no knowledge or writing whatsoever in contempt. Always approach your reading with a spirit of humility and receptivity, accepting the book as a gift and trusting that you can benefit from something in its pages.

Then, finally, take Tippet's advice and "define your curiosity" so that you might never forget that we read so as to curate a conversation—between ourselves and the book's author—about the art of being human.

For to read with any other purpose would suggest a profound problem of the soul.

Trust me, I know.

13

Choosing What to Read

A FEW YEARS AGO, the communications committee at my church decided to begin uploading my weekly sermons and distributing them as a podcast. This development has brought me in touch with many people I might otherwise have never met, and it has also led to my hearing from old friends with whom I haven't spoken in years.

Recently, one such friend texted me that a sermon in which I'd referenced Fyodor Dostoyevsky's *The Idiot* had been staying with her. "Beauty will save the world," I opened that sermon by saying, which is a line from the novel spoken by Dostoyevsky's protagonist, Prince Myshkin.

"I have been thinking about that," my friend texted me. "And about how true it is. You're right, seeing the beauty in something is always more compelling than just being told how beautiful it is." I thanked my friend for the kind words and told her I was glad the sermon had been meaningful to her. "How do you pick which books you read?" she texted back. "In the few sermons I have listened to, I've heard you reference five different books. Some of them fiction, some not. How do you choose?"

What my friend was asking me was a question I often hear from aspiring pastor-readers, and it is a very important one.

And the answer is: I just choose.

Now, I recognize how insufficient that answer sounds—and I will attempt to be more helpful and more precise in what follows—but it first bears mentioning that in my personal philosophy of reading, reading by faith and not by sight is the only proper way to read. In *The Pleasures of Reading in an Age of Distraction*, Alan Jacobs refers to this approach as reading "by whim," meaning, reading whatever happens to be piquing our curiosity or our fascination in a given moment.[1] Jacobs calls this "whim" because, who knows what—or when, or why—something piques our curiosity or our fascination?

Take, for example, my own experience with John Irving's *A Prayer for Owen Meany*. About fifteen years ago I bought a paperback copy of the book for a dollar at a used bookstore. I left the store positively elated, having scored a remarkable bargain on a book that numerous people had told me I was going to love.

I went straight back to my apartment that day, lay down on my sofa, began to read the novel, and . . . *nothing*. The book was dull and lifeless, more impenetrable than concrete. But because so many people had told me how wonderful the book was, I soldiered on. And over the course of the next few days, I (laboriously) read about 150 pages.

Then, finally, I gave up. I put the book on my shelf, and I moved on to something new.

Throughout the next several years, though, I'd regularly find myself in discussion with bookish friends who often cited *Owen Meany* as a favorite, and I'd often leave those conversations with a renewed commitment to giving the novel yet another try.

And always I'd make it to about page 150; and always I'd then give up. I figure this happened at least four times over the course of seven years, maybe more. For whatever reason, even though I knew I was supposed to like it, I just didn't. I just *couldn't*.

Years later, though, while browsing my shelves looking for a different book, I came across the spine of that old copy of *Owen Meany*, the same copy I had stopped and started so many times in the past. And this day, for whatever reason, it seemed to be reaching for me, calling out to me, beckoning me to open it.

And so I did. I pulled it down, opened to the first page, and began to read—*with no intention of actually reading the whole book.* This time, though, *for whatever reason,* I couldn't put the book down. Each page turned effortlessly into the next, each scene giving way compellingly to the one that followed it; and while I at first stood reading by my bookshelf, soon enough I moved to my reading chair, aware that even though I had come to the shelf looking for one book, *this* was the book that I would now be reading.

I finished the book—all 617 pages—less than two weeks later, staying up into the wee hours of the morning many nights because I couldn't put it down. And as I read Irving's penultimate sentence—". . . they were the forces we didn't have the faith to feel, they were the forces we failed to believe in"—I felt the unbelievable force of personal victory.

—

Now, you'll note that I used the phrase "for whatever reason" several times in telling that story. I did so very intentionally. The "for whatever reason" element in the story *is* the "whim" Alan Jacobs is talking about. The "for whatever reason" element is the impetus for readers who "read by faith and not by sight." The "for whatever reason" is the substance of things we as pastor-readers hope for, the evidence of directional forces unseen.

Above, I referred to this as my "philosophy of reading," but it would be more precise to call it a *pneumatology* of reading, because I deeply believe that the Holy Spirit plays a central (though intrinsically mysterious) role in directing us as pastor-readers toward what—and when, and why—to read.

I have no real *method* for choosing what to read, because even if I tell you what books have been helpful for me and why, it doesn't follow that these books will be helpful for *you* (or even if they are, that they will be helpful for the same reasons). Instead, the key to choosing what to read as a pastor-reader is simply to be endlessly curious and to be hopelessly committed, and from there, to trust that the right books *will* call to us—not we to them—at precisely the right time.

This "call" can take the form of a recommendation from a friend; a casual jaunt through a bookstore; a review you've read on the Internet; a book you've found forlorn in some nameless café; a spine you discover on your own bookshelf—the call can come from anywhere, at any time.

There are, after all, an endless number of portals into Narnia, and the only way to ensure that you won't get in is by actively trying.

—

Now, having said all that, I do want to say a word about the breakdown of what we read. By which I mean, what genres we should read and in what manner.

You've likely noticed that throughout this book I have referenced many works of fiction. This, too, has been intentional. It's not that I read more fiction than I do nonfiction—as you'll soon see, I don't. (Not even close.)

Instead, I have intentionally been referencing novels because, as pastors, our guild has a notoriously bad habit of devaluing fiction, conceiving of it as "made-up stories" that therefore have nothing "real" to teach us.

This is a terrible misunderstanding of both the power and the function of fiction. For fiction helps us understand others and the wider world in deeper, more *experiential* ways than nonfiction ever can—even if we are never able to fully articulate that understanding. As James K. A. Smith writes, "Stories [fiction] have reasons of which Reason knows nothing."[2]

This was a crucial insight for C. S. Lewis into the very nature of Christian faith itself. The story, Lewis found, has more binding power and spiritual vitality than the doctrinal beliefs that derive from it. For when we are "in" a story, we are "knowing" in an immediate, experiential way, whereas when we are reading nonfiction, we are at a remove from that which we are reading about, "knowing" it in a more abstract and less immediate kind of way.[3]

Now, make no mistake: both ways of knowing are necessary for us as pastor-readers, but I foreground fiction because of how regularly we pastors leave it unattended. A 2013 Barna study, for example, found that pastors buy more books per year than the average person—but less *fiction* than the average person.[4]

This is a problem. Because it is *fiction* that most stretches us and expands us as pastor-readers; it is *fiction* that equips us to sense inarticulable things lurking at levels unseen in our membership; it is *fiction* that helps us intuit what is really going on underneath the headlines and the hot takes that dominate the current media landscape.

Yes, I understand through nonfiction like *The Culture of Narcissism* and *Habits of the Heart* and *The Age of Disruption* and *Alienated America* that unfettered capitalism and hyperindividualism are together decimating the "social capital" necessary for maintaining healthy and thriving local communities; but I understand this in a far more elemental way by reading Upton Sinclair's novel *The Jungle*—or better yet, by reading Steinbeck's *The Grapes of Wrath* or Chinua Achebe's *Things Fall Apart.*

The point here being: To be a pastor-reader does not require reading only fiction, but it most certainly requires reading a lot *of* fiction. Because only through fiction can we understand things on that spiritual level that Saint Paul describes as "too deep for words."

Recently, a pastor friend in Florida texted me that he'd just read and loved *Gilead*—it was the first novel he had read since high school—and, after thanking me for the recommendation, he said he was going to order *Home*, the next book in the *Gilead* saga, and he asked whether I thought it was ethical to use his church credit card to make the purchase. "Is it really a ministerial expense?" he asked. "Like, is it really *for* ministry?"

"Yes," I responded. "In ways you'll never fully know."

—

So that's my advice on fiction: read it. Read a lot of it. Then read some more of it. And all the while, trust that what you're reading is slowly forming a deeper kind of knowledge in you than you'll ever be able to fully articulate. Without this knowledge, your ability to discern and intuit and respond to things taking place at deeper, lower registers of the human condition will be necessarily reduced.

Meanwhile, when it comes to reading nonfiction, my advice is almost exactly the same—yet for almost the exact opposite reason. We should also read nonfiction as much—and as widely—as we can, but *un*like fiction, we read nonfiction to better understand and articulate things. That is, unlike with fiction, we *expect* through reading nonfiction to "know more" about whatever it is we are reading about. We expect through reading nonfiction to be able to talk more informedly and more assuredly on any given topic.

Now, please don't misunderstand: this doesn't mean that we read nonfiction instrumentally—we don't read *this* book, or *this* article, or *this* essay for the strict purpose of putting it into *this* sermon, or using it during *this* pastoral visit; with nonfiction, too, we are "filling the reservoir"—but we *do* read nonfiction with the aim of better comprehending a given topic and being better informed about it.

This is why nonfiction lends itself, in a way that fiction does not, to the reading of many things at the same time. Unlike fiction, which works on us at "subterranean levels" and which requires us therefore to "stay in the story" in order to be maximally formed and affected by it, nonfiction works on us primarily at an intellectual level, which means we can often benefit from "getting away" for a while from each work of nonfiction.

In other words, with nonfiction, we often need time to process and distill the ideas and information we are reading, because seldom does such knowledge fully penetrate *in the immediate moment of reading*. It usually takes time for the material to take root, for it to find appropriately fertile mental soil in which it can blossom and mature. For that reason, having several items going at once—that is, reading several different nonfiction books on a wide variety of topics *all at once*—provides us with the kind of intellectual breaks necessary for slowly comprehending each of the different things we are reading about.

Meanwhile, when we do this, our brains naturally attempt to synthesize material from the various things we are reading, our minds looking to make connections between seemingly unrelated and disparate phenomena. This process helps us form unexpected insights while slowly prodding us toward greater understanding of the various things we are reading.

Thus, while I recommend reading one work of fiction at a time, I recommend reading several works of nonfiction simultaneously—the more varied the subject matter, the better—breaking each book up as the Spirit leads.

Now, I do recognize that some people are wired in such a way that starting a book and putting it down before finishing—so as to pick up another—is nearly impossible. So great is the sense of obligation in such individuals to finish what has been started that the thought alone of reading several books at a time causes panic and palpitations.

I'm not saying that to be a pastor-reader you *have* to read in a way that defies your given temperament and constitution. That would fly directly in the face of "whim," of my own pneumatology of reading. But I *am* saying that if you're at least open to giving it a try, the stop-start nature of reading many different nonfiction books at a time may begin enriching you and making you more conversant on several different things all at once, in a way less likely if you were reading only one thing at a time.

In sum, there is a nearly inexhaustible list of genres from which to benefit as a pastor-reader: novels and novellas, current events and biographies, short stories and essays, poetry collections and nature writing, memoirs and travel narratives, newspapers and magazines— the list is almost infinite.

In fact, one of my favorite sermons of the past several years, written during the early days of the 2020 COVID-19 lockdown, used as a central motif the line "The walls became the world all around" from Maurice Sendak's children's book *Where the Wild Things Are*. In other words, if we simply follow it where it listeth, there is no telling where the whimsical Spirit of "for whatever reason" may blow us. For, in the end, the key to being a pastor-reader isn't knowing what *to* read; it's simply trusting what will happen to us if we *do* read.

So takeaway number 4, then, for how to be a pastor-reader is this: trust that there is beauty to be found in all sorts of books—in many cases, in books that we, of our own volition, might never even think to open—and then trust that, upon reading such books, we will further appreciate the degree to which beauty really will save the world.

How to Mark and File What You've Read

I SURMISE THAT by this point many are wondering whether this book will ever address digital reading. The answer to that question is, yes, it will. Right now, as a matter of fact.

But be forewarned: what I have to say about digital reading will be short and sweet, because this chapter isn't really about digital reading; it's about how to mark what we've read and how to file it for later use.

However, because "marking" and "filing" necessarily impinge on the question of genre and format, a quick word on digital reading is now appropriate. (And by "digital reading," I simply mean "reading things on the Internet.") Like many of you, I well remember the halcyon years of the early Internet when, because of our sudden access to so many sites and so much new information, people would often say, "People are reading now more than ever!" To some degree, this was true—if by "reading" we mean "looking at words on the Internet."

Today, though, virtually all scholars and research scientists agree that just because someone is spending a lot of time on the Internet, and just because someone is clicking on numerous news stories per day, does not mean that the individual is actually *reading* what he or she is looking at.

Instead, 55 percent of all page-views get fewer than fifteen seconds of a viewer's time, and of those fifteen seconds, 69 percent of them is spent viewing what is on the left side of the page and only 30 percent viewing what is on the right.[1] In other words, whatever we are doing when we are looking at digital sites, it's certainly not "reading" in the word's most fundamental sense.

This accords with a study Nicholas Carr references in *The Shallows: What the Internet Is Doing to Our Brains*, where the research/consulting firm nGenera makes the case that "Digital immersion . . . has affected the way [we] absorb information. [We] don't necessarily read a page from left to right and from top to bottom. [We] . . . instead skip around, scanning for pertinent information of interest."[2]

This is a problem. And the problem is not so much with the technology itself (though the technology gives rise *to* the problem) as with the way this distractable and fragmented manner of "reading" affects us personally, temperamentally, and cognitively. Writes Carr: "We seem to have arrived . . . at an important juncture in our intellectual and cultural history, a moment of transition between two very different modes of thinking. What we're trading away in return for the riches of the Net—and only a curmudgeon would refuse to see the riches—is . . . 'our old linear thought process.' Calm, focused, undistracted, the linear mind is being pushed aside by a new kind of mind that wants and needs to take in and dole out information in short, disjointed, often overlapping bursts—the faster, the better."[3]

Thus, my reasons for discouraging digital reading for pastor-readers has nothing to do with an aversion to technology; instead, it has everything to do with the traits and manners necessary for members of our particular guild. As pastors, we are not called to be anxious, distracted, disjointed thinkers; if the energy we radiate to those in our care suggests a constant sense of urgency and a givenness to irritability, we will fail at our principal role: to be patient and unhurried shepherds of our people.

In *The Contemplative Pastor*, Eugene Peterson quotes a line from *Moby Dick* about the calmed, poised nature of a harpooner over against the frenzied nature of all other members of a ship's crew, particularly its oarsmen. Peterson uses the line ("to ensure the greatest efficiency in the dart, the harpooners of this world must start to their feet out of idleness and not out of toil") to describe the necessary disposition of the pastor. Peterson then explains, "Our culture publicizes . . . the big, the multitudinous, the noisy. It is, then, a strategic necessity that pastors deliberately ally themselves with the quiet, poised harpooners, and not leap, frenzied, to the oars. There is far more need that we develop the skills of the harpooner than the muscles of the oarsman."[4]

Taking Peterson's caution to heart, it seems clear that the scattered, distractable reading currently taking place on the Internet is turning the culture around us into a cacophony of further frenzied oarsmen; and for that reason, we as pastor-readers are well advised to hone our quiet, poised harpooning skills principally through analogue reading.

—

Now, a few quick caveats on this before we proceed.

First, I want to assure you that I am no Luddite. I carry around a smartphone in my pocket, just as you do; and I agree with Carr, that only a curmudgeon would refuse to see the riches made possible by the Internet. I personally have online subscriptions to both the *Wall Street Journal* and the *New York Times*, and I read them both daily—on my phone.

My point is not to dissuade you from *all* digital engagement; it's simply to dissuade you from construing the digital reading you do on your smartphone (or laptop) to be the same *kind* of reading you do as a pastor-reader, for these are qualitatively different kinds of reading.

Second, what I have said above strictly pertains to online reading and has nothing to do with Kindles or other such portable readers.

While I do not own a portable reader, I know them to be—and studies have found them to be—just as effective at sharpening a reader's linear-thinking skills and a reader's deep-reading capacities as traditional print formats are.[5]

—

With those caveats aside, a word on how to mark our readings and how to file what we've read. I mentioned earlier that my first experience marking a book (outside of an academic setting) was with Ha Jin's *Waiting*. And while I have sentimental feelings toward that book on account of those markings, the truth is, I cringe when I see them.

Put differently, I am horrified by *how* I marked that book. Rather than underline key sentences, I bracketed them. And rather than differentiate the significance of memorable passages through a combination of check marks (important), stars (very important), and exclamation points (*don't you dare forget this!*)—which is my current system—I used only stars and exclamation points, seemingly interchangeably. Which is to say, my markings were both obtrusive and inconsistent, breaking up the flow of the prose while sending mixed signals about what was important and why.

Today, I can pull a book from my shelf at random and know precisely when I read it vis-à-vis my evolution as a book-marker. For instance, when I pull Sue Monk Kidd's *The Secret Life of Bees* and Ann Patchett's *Bel Canto* from my shelves, I can see, evidenced by the copious number of brackets and by the complete absence of check marks, that I was clearly still in that earliest stage.

When I pull down, say, Thomas Merton's *Seven Storey Mountain* or Annie Dillard's *Pilgrim at Tinker Creek*, I see that at that point I had been marking my books for at least a year or two, because the brackets are gone and I am suddenly overly dependent on underlining. (My God, the underlining!) The evolution goes on, but I don't want to belabor the point.

It is only when I pick up my copy of Wendell Berry's *The Memory of Old Jack* that I see the first signs of my transition into the method I currently use, and this is not due to my own markings in the book but rather due to the markings of Neil Dunnavant, the man who gave me the book.

Neil was the executive pastor at the Presbyterian church in which I interned during divinity school, and more than any pastor I have ever met, Neil embodies the ethos of the pastor-reader. Neil reads constantly, voraciously. He was my first real pastoral mentor, my first champion, and, though we seldom talk these days, I still count him as one of my most cherished friends.

Neil and I bonded over books during my initial interview at the church, and for the three years I served there he and I were inseparable, each conversation leading us always back to books, as all roads to Rome. To this day, Neil periodically forwards me a list of books that his book club has been reading; no note is ever attached because no explanation is necessary. *I know you'll never tire of hearing about what I'm reading*, the email suggests.

And he's right. And here's why I mention Neil now: When I first read Neil's copy of *The Memory of Old Jack* all those years ago, I was taken not only by the beauty of Berry's story but also by the clarity of Neil's notation system. Rather than the haphazard markings in my own books, Neil's markings were precise. He used small, unobtrusive check marks. He was reserved in his usage of underlines and sparing in his use of stars. He did not use exclamation marks at all—which, as I said above, are a form of notation that I continue to value—but nonetheless, Neil clearly had a system, something I as yet did not. Moreover, Neil's markings were so *neat* (as opposed to the sloppiness of my own), and his margin notes were so economical in comparison to my own verbose ramblings.

It is no exaggeration to say that seeing Neil's system changed everything about the way I went about marking my own books. And to this day, if you pick up a copy of a book I am reading, you will find Neil's influence penciled throughout the pages.

I tell you all of this so as to say: If you aren't currently reading with a pencil in hand, you need to be; marking what you read is not a technique useful only in school. Making notations in books remains just as useful—if not *more* useful—when you read of your own volition. This goes not only for nonfiction but also for fiction. And if you don't already have a notation system, develop one. There is no right or wrong system to have—you are free to tailor your system to fit your own needs and personality—but make sure that you have one, and make sure it is consistent.

Finally, dare to be like Machiavelli and "speak back" to the text, making margin notes that will help you later remember how you "experienced" the reading conversation. But when you do make such notes, be like my friend Neil, not like me. That is, be concise in your notes and be judicious in how often you use them. After all, no one likes a conversation partner who never shuts up and who, even worse, takes five sentences to say what could be said in a few words.

—

So, enough about marking books; a word now on how to file what we have marked. Many years ago, Alex Lockridge, my dear friend whom I mentioned in chapter 4, who was then an associate minister at my church in Kentucky and who is now the church's senior pastor, popped into my office to inquire about this very issue. "You use so many literary references in your sermons," he said, "and I have been wondering: Do you have a system for that? Like, how do you remember all the things you read?"

I told Alex about "the reservoir," and about how the best way to read is to read without knowing how the reading might ultimately benefit us. Then I told him that, no, I didn't have a system—that I just essentially remembered things; that the references I use just "come to me"—and that, when they do, I go back to the book from which they came and track them down.

As I told Alex this, I could see how much of a letdown the answer was. He responded by telling me that he was able to do something similar when it came to numbers, but that his memory was not nearly so precise when it came to reading.

I have been haunted by that conversation ever since. For here was one of the first people ever to seek me out for "pastor-reader" advice—long before I'd ever begun thinking of my own reading in such terms—and I'd had nothing substantive to give him in response.

Ever since that day, I have dedicated myself to refining my own method and to having a more practical answer for anyone interested in knowing how I retain what I read. And like my method for marking books, so too has my "filing" method evolved over the years. Today, the method I use is breathtakingly simple, but it benefits me greatly.

And here it is: Upon finishing a book, I transcribe every checked and starred and exclamated passage into a single Microsoft Word document.

That's it. My expert advice is: Mark your books, then transcribe the passages that you've marked into a single word-processing document.

Now, typically, when I explain this simple method, people ask whether I file each passage under a certain theme, like grace, or sin, or forgiveness. No, I don't. Because, as I've said before, the right image or the right quotation can't be forced to fit where it doesn't really fit. Just because a quote has to do with forgiveness does not mean it's the right quote for what we are saying about forgiveness *right now*.

Thus, the benefit of the ever-growing document is that it is searchable yet not overly prescriptive. It helps you find a quote or a passage that you only vaguely recall, yet it meanwhile militates against the temptation to force the wrong quote into the wrong place. For instance, I don't search "forgiveness" in my Word document and then look through each result that features the word; instead, I remember, say, a description of guilt and condemnation that once gripped me in *Les Misérables*, and then I search "Les Misérables" or "Jean Valjean" or "convict," and that helps me narrow my search down to the precise reference I am looking for: "Liberation is not deliverance. A convict may leave the galleys behind, but not his condemnation." This quote would not work for just *any* point a preacher is making about forgiveness. But for a point specifically pertaining to the way our human need for forgiveness hounds us no matter how hard we run from our guilt, the quote works perfectly.

Meanwhile, the other great benefit of this system is that if I want a quick overview of a book that I haven't read in many years, I can simply pull up the entries from that book, read them in about ten minutes, and thereby remember all the nuggets of wisdom that were so nourishing when first I read that particular book.

This is a way to refine the reservoir—a way to stir the water, so to speak—so as to further ensure that when the proper moment comes, our reservoirs runneth over.

—

It's not very flashy, I know. But there it is. And it works.

So, in the end, takeaway number 5 for how to be a pastor-reader is this: try to read as much material off-line as possible. Digital reading has been demonstrably proven to lead to disjointed thinking, increased anxiousness, and heightened impulsivity, while traditional analogue reading has been demonstrably proven to sharpen one's reasoning skills, focus one's mind, and aid one's better judgment.

Then, after committing to more traditional forms of reading, develop a system for marking and notating that which you read, and make sure your system is concise and consistent.

Finally, make certain to transcribe all passages you have marked into a single, searchable document via your preferred word processor, such as Microsoft Word or Apple Pages.

If you'll do these simple things, your reservoir will continue to be filled and you will have readier access to the quotes and images and allusions that will benefit your sermons and your studies. More importantly, though, you will have ready access to the darts necessary for harpooning the whales that daily threaten the oarsmen of your church, and what's more, you will have the calm and the poise to ensure the greatest efficiency in the dart.

15

Reading Scripture as a Pastor-Reader

DURING A WORSHIP SERVICE a few months ago, amid a time of deep societal unrest, I prayed these words: "Right now we are making a proper mess of it, oh God. Right now we are beating our plowshares into swords and turning our pruning hooks into daggers. Right now we are cheering on the harsh words that stir up anger and looking with antipathy upon the kind words that turneth away wrath. Right now we are disdainful of the truth, because, like Pilate, it's not the truth we care about but instead our own personal agendas."

In response to that prayer—in fact, in response to this excerpt from it—I received a text after the worship service from a church member asking me for a copy. Then, a day later, I received this email from him in response:

> Austin, thank you for sending me a copy of your prayer. It is and will continue to be an inspiration to me. Among the words that I found most helpful are these:
>
> "Right now we are beating our plowshares into swords and turning our pruning hooks into daggers."
>
> "Right now we are cheering on the harsh words that stir up anger and looking with antipathy upon the kind words that turneth away wrath."

"Right now we are disdainful of the truth, because, like Pilate, it's
not the truth we care about but instead our own personal agendas."
Powerful, insightful, and informative words. Amen and Amen!

I bring up this prayer, and I quote this response, in order to make
this crucial point: the aspects of the prayer that so moved this church
member—the parts that spoke to him on such a deep level that he
later sought me out to ask for a copy—are words that are *bathed* in
scriptural allusion and imagery.

The first line, of course, uses language and imagery from Isaiah
2:4. The second line riffs on language from Proverbs 15:1. And the
third line is a direct allusion to the confrontation between Jesus and
Pontius Pilate that takes place in John 18.

I did not intentionally use *any* of this language and imagery in my
prayer; instead, these words simply *came out of me* as I sat down to
write it. Moreover, the reason *these particular words* came out is owing
to how—and to how often—I read the Scriptures. I read the Bible
daily, and because I read the Bible not only for instructional and devo-
tional purposes but also for purposes of embeddedness and wonder,
certain phrases and cadences and images become deeply implanted
within me, such that they later spring forth in ways that—and at times
when—I don't necessarily intend for them to.

That's reason number 1 for telling this story: to point out how daily
Scripture reading can eventuate in biblical language embedding itself
within us and coming out when least we expect it. I also tell this story
to point out that the reason *these particular lines* from my prayer—as
opposed to any of the lines around them—stuck with this church
member is entirely owing to the mysterious power of scriptural language, the way Scripture's poetic and inspired nature evokes in hearers an elevated sense of resonance and transcendence.

In short, the Spirit *always* has the capacity to "quickeneth," as Jesus
tells his disciples in John 6:63, but, in my experience, the odds of our

pastoral words being quickened are greatly heightened when we use language and imagery that derive directly from the Holy Scriptures.

——

In *Echoes of Scripture in the Letters of Paul* and then later in *Reading Backwards*, New Testament scholar and former dean of Duke Divinity School Richard Hays argues that Paul and other New Testament writers quoted Hebrew Scripture regularly and knowingly, but they often referenced Hebrew Scripture *un*knowingly, too. Citing countless examples, Hays makes the case that, for these early Christian writers (Paul being the foremost example), the Scriptures were *so deeply embedded* within them that these language forms became default expressions in their daily parlance, the lingua franca through which they expressed and articulated this new Christian "way."

So much so that they sometimes failed even to notice when they'd just used it. "The vocabulary and cadences of Scripture," Hays writes, "are imprinted deeply on Paul's mind, and the great stories of Israel continue to serve for him as a fund of symbols and metaphors that condition his perception of the world, of God's promised deliverance of his people, and of his own identity and calling. His faith, in short, is one whose articulation is inevitably intertextual in character."[1]

N. T. Wright, making a similar case in *Paul: A Biography*, claims, "Paul has something else of which fewer people, even in his own world, could boast. He gives every impression of having swallowed the Bible whole. He moves with polished ease between Genesis and the Psalms, between Deuteronomy and Isaiah. He knows how the story works, its heights and depths, its twists and turns. He can make complex allusions with a flick of the pen and produce puns and other wordplays across the languages."[2]

I quote this passage from Wright for two reasons. First, like Hays, Wright is here making the case that an immersion in the Scriptures gives a Christian teacher and preacher (in this case, the apostle Paul) a certain felicity with the scriptural material, an ease with using its language and imagery in daily discourse.

More important, though, I quote this passage to show how Wright, himself, *while writing this exact paragraph*, unintentionally proves his own point. Note how, in describing Paul's familiarity with Scripture, Wright describes Paul as "having swallowed the Bible whole." Then consider *these* words from Jeremiah 15:16:

> When your words came, *I ate them*;
> > they were my joy and my heart's delight. (NIV 2011,
> > emphasis mine)

In other words, Wright himself—in a passage about how Paul uses biblical allusions to make his various points—uses a biblical allusion *to make his own point*, seemingly without knowing that this is what he's just done.

To be fair, as I did with the above prayer, Wright likely realized what he'd done *after the fact*; but the takeaway for our purposes is that, in the moment of verbal creation, the allusion seems to have just "come to him." It was just *there*, and this on account of Wright's utter familiarity with the entire scriptural corpus, the way that Wright daily "eats" the Word and the way that the Word has therefore become deeply embedded within him.

—

So, that is my first word of advice when it comes to approaching our scriptural reading as pastor-readers: read for *embeddedness*, for the ever-increasing capacity to use elevated language that carries with it the maximal potential for being "quickened" by the Spirit. For, as I said, scriptural language has a certain poetry to it, a beauty that strikes a mysterious chord deep within a listener's heart, often evoking in him or her a sense of reverence and awe. This was what the above-referenced church member experienced during my prayer, and this was what I experienced when reading the line quoted above from N. T. Wright. And remember, on account of such embeddedness, even when we don't *know* that we have just used language or imagery that derives from Scripture, the power that such language and imagery wield remains the same.

Therefore, read Scripture with an awareness that the more you read it, the more it will become for you like a second, albeit much deeper, language. And make this potentiality of language cultivation of paramount importance to you when reading Scripture, rather than just something you see as an ancillary benefit. For this approach to reading Scripture truly does help us as pastors tap into a tremendous source of rhetorical power.

In *Reading Backwards*, Hays recounts how the playwright Arthur Miller, early in his career, would often sit at his typewriter and, while reading the words aloud, transcribe the collected works of Shakespeare, over and over and over again, with the express purpose of getting Shakespeare's language and cadence and imagery so deeply embedded within him that when he turned to write his own plays, the spirit of Shakespeare would be lurking just underneath each word and each scene he wrote.[3]

So should we as pastor-readers be doing with the Holy Scriptures. We should be daily *eating* the words, that they might become embedded within us and thereby find their way into everything we write and say and do.

—

In *Reading for Preaching*, Neal Plantinga wisely writes at the book's outset, "The preacher is, first, an absorbed reader of the Bible and a champion of it among us . . . nothing I write about a program of general reading supplants this."[4]

I agree with Plantinga wholeheartedly; nothing I have written in this book about a program of general reading supplants the pastoral priority of reading Scripture. Unlike Plantinga, however, I include this same caveat at my book's *end* because I've wanted in this book to foreground the pastoral significance of reading things *other* than the Bible.

As Alan Jacobs says in *A Theology of Reading*, so I say as well: "Almost no one seems to have considered reading of non-Biblical texts a theologically significant activity. And yet only if reading *is* a theologically significant activity can many of the counsels I am making in this book be justified."[5]

But that being said, while my intention with this book has been to encourage pastors to read things *other* than the Bible, I certainly don't want pastors to read other things in *place* of the Bible. I hope it goes without saying, but I think that the Bible is the *sine qua non* of books, the divinely inspired word of God, the most important and most life-giving anthology ever compiled. As such, I read the Bible daily for devotion and for preparation, for instruction and for reproof, for inspiration and for edification, for salvation and for sanctification.

Meanwhile, though, I also read it for *wonder*.

And that is how I want this book to end: with an encouragement to you as an aspiring pastor-reader to approach the Holy Scriptures with the same sort of wonder with which you approach all other powerful works of literature.

Now, please don't misunderstand me. I'm not saying that the Bible is *only* literature. But I *am* saying that we do the Bible a grave disservice when we think of it as something *other* than literature. Wheaton professor Leland Ryken, in his book *How to Read the Bible as Literature*, makes this very point: "My claim is simply that the literary approach is one necessary way to read and interpret the Bible, an approach that has been unjustifiably neglected. Despite that neglect, the literary approach builds at every turn on what biblical scholars have done to recover the original, intended meaning of the biblical text."[6]

For example, recently I was reading Acts 10, the story of Peter's encounter with Cornelius the Roman centurion. I don't know how many times I have read this passage, always taking away from it something about the new covenant, or about the breaking down of barriers, or about the inclusivity of Christ, or about the power of the Spirit. But as I read the chapter on that day, I was suddenly floored by the realization that such transformations *are* possible.

These things *do* happen. As human beings, we really *are* capable of having our entire understanding of reality upended; of having our deep-seated prejudices exposed to ourselves; of having our petty preoccupations with ourselves and our own ideas radically overturned.

And with this realization, I suddenly realized, too, that such transformations are never *welcome* in the moment. Instead, as Flannery O'Connor puts it, such transformations occur only through "violent" acts of grace, a type of grace for which we are almost always ungrateful in the given moment.

Like Peter is in Acts chapter 10.

In our usual reading of this passage, we are often so eager to take from it an idyllic message on the power of the Spirit to unify or on the theological significance of gentiles being "grafted in," that we entirely overlook how profoundly human and *un*idyllic Peter's own response was in the moment of encounter.

This is what I mean when I say we should read Scripture for wonder. I mean we should read Scripture with the aim of seeing ourselves in the text; I mean we should read it with the aim of having our sense of creation's complexity expanded; I mean we should read it with the aim of not just taking away a lesson from it, but taking away a greater sense of life from it, too.

"He had a strange and peculiar way of judging things. I suspect that he acquired it from the Gospel." This is Victor Hugo describing Bishop Myriel in *Les Misérables*.

I suspect that he acquired it from the Gospel.

This is what happens when we eat the Scriptures, when we daily read the Bible with a sense of wonder.

We are shaped by it.

Our lives are transformed by it.
Our very humanity is drawn up into it.
Our very natures are perfected by it.

In short, we are saved—and it's an ongoing salvation that we continue to *acquire* through our reading.

—

I said early in this book that, to my mind, two individuals stand out as pastor-readers par excellence, Eugene Peterson and the apostle Paul.

I have cited at length why I include Peterson in this elite category, but I close the book now by explaining why I also include the apostle Paul. In the same section of Wright's *Paul* from which I quoted above, Wright, now pointing to Paul's fluency with *non*-Jewish literature and philosophy, writes, "He knows the ideas. . . . He knows the technical terms, the philosophical schemes that probe the mysteries of the universe and the inner workings of human beings," and then Wright goes on to say that, were anyone to suddenly wax eloquent on matters of Stoicism or Epicureanism or on the writings of folks like Cicero, Paul "would be able to engage such a person on his own terms."

Wright then summarizes the point he is making by saying, "Paul is thus completely at home in the worlds of both Jewish story and non-Jewish philosophy."[7] Or, for the point *I'm* trying to make: Paul is a *pastor-reader*, someone whose daily immersion in wide, curious reading orients his entire way of living and moving and having his being in the world.

Like a true pastor-reader, Paul has so deeply read the Scriptures, and has so widely (and charitably) read materials *other* than the Scriptures, that he is thereby able to speak knowingly and wisely and illuminatingly on all manner of things—and what's more, when he opens his mouth to speak, no matter what he happens to be speaking *about*, the cadences and rhythms and language of Scripture undergird his every word.

In the end, this is what a pastor-reader ultimately is: a pastor like Paul, someone whose deep commitment to reading emanates—*exudes*—from everything he or she does or says or touches or teaches.

Writing to Timothy, his beloved disciple, Paul, the pastor-reader par excellence, says: "Do your best to come to me soon. . . . When you come, bring my books."[8] When I read these words, I hear echoes of Neil Dunnavant sending me emails with his recent reading list; and I hear echoes of James Bennett coming to my office to tell me about what reading *Gilead* has meant to him; and I hear echoes of Paul Sims leaving books on my desk each Christmas Eve, all of them simply marked "Love, Paul."

In short, when I read these words from Paul to Timothy, I think of how deeply embedded the mark of such wise and literate mentors is on my life, and I wonder at the generous Spirit who saw fit to graft my story into theirs.

I am not only a better reader and a better pastor because of them; I am also a far better man. Each of these men has a presence and a light that points others toward an altogether different and better world.

And I not only suspect, but I *know*, that each of them acquired it from the gospel.

Postscript

I WAS RECENTLY WALKING through downtown Greenville with my family when I happened to notice a young woman, likely an undergraduate student from Furman University, sitting alone on a bench with a cup of coffee beside her and Elizabeth Strout's *Olive Kitteridge* in her hand. Suddenly, my heart swelled with gratitude, because, having read and loved this book, I knew how much this experience was likely going to mean to her.

When you are a reader, you long for others to know and to experience the same kind of joy from books that you, yourself, have known.

When you are a reader, you long for others to enter the same fascinating worlds that you, yourself, have once entered, even if you know you'll never likely get to discuss these worlds with one another.

When you are a reader, you long for others to long for books the same way that you do.

And in the end, that is why I have written this book. I have written it because I long for you to long for books the same way that I do.

It's not only that I believe that reading will make you a better pastor—which I do—but it's because I believe that reading will make you a better person, too.

A happier person.

A more grateful person.

A more content person.

Therefore, as I sit now in my reading chair, my family still asleep and Carl Honore's *In Praise of Slowness* in my hands, I offer a brief prayer that you too might slow down with me so as to become a pastor-reader, thereby entering some of the same fascinating worlds and thereby experiencing some of the same great joys that I, myself, have entered and known.

And while I know it is unlikely that you and I will ever meet to discuss such things, the knowledge alone that you have taken the time to slow down and read this particular book fills me with great gratitude.

And thus, with Shakespeare I say unto you: "I can no other answer make but thanks, and thanks, and ever thanks."

Notes

FOREWORD

1. Craig Dykstra, "A Way of Seeing: Imagination and the Pastoral Life," *Christian Century*, April 8, 2008, 26.

2. Dykstra, "A Way of Seeing," 26.

3. Dykstra, "A Way of Seeing," 30.

CHAPTER 1

1. C. S. Lewis, *Surprised by Joy: The Shape of My Early Life* (Orlando: Harcourt, 1955), 16–18.

2. James K. A. Smith, *Imagining the Kingdom: How Worship Works* (Grand Rapids: Baker Academic, 2013), 136.

3. M. Craig Barnes, *Diary of a Pastor's Soul: The Holy Moments in a Life of Ministry* (Grand Rapids: Brazos, 2020), 11. See also M. Craig Barnes, *The Pastor as Minor Poet: Texts and Subtexts in the Ministerial Life* (Grand Rapids: Eerdmans, 2009), 48–53.

4. Maryanne Wolf, *Reader, Come Home: The Reading Brain in a Digital World* (New York: HarperCollins, 2018), 62.

5. See Wolf, *Reader, Come Home*, especially 35–68. See also Maryanne Wolf, *Proust and the Squid* (New York: HarperCollins, 2007).

6. Wolf, *Reader, Come Home*, 35–68.

7. Nicholas Carr, *The Shallows: What the Internet Is Doing to Our Brains* (New York: Norton, 2011), 34.

8. James K. A. Smith, *You Are What You Love: The Spiritual Power of Habit* (Grand Rapids: Brazos, 2016), 27–55.

9. Wolf, *Reader, Come Home*, 61 (emphasis added).

10. Wolf, *Reader, Come Home*, 103.

CHAPTER 2

1. Research on this varies. For a helpful overview, see Julie Beck, "Why We Forget Most of the Books We Read," *Atlantic*, January 26, 2018, https://www.theatlantic.com/science/archive/2018/01/what-was-this-article-about-again/551603/.

2. For helpful overviews, see Nicholas Carr, *The Shallows: What the Internet Is Doing to Our Brains* (New York: Norton, 2011); Maryanne Wolf, *Proust and the Squid* (New York: HarperCollins, 2007); and Maryanne Wolf, *Reader, Come Home: The Reading Brain in a Digital World* (New York: HarperCollins, 2018). For an overview specifically pertaining to fiction, see Keith Oatley, *Such Stuff as Dreams: The Psychology of Fiction* (Malden, MA: Wiley-Blackwell, 2011).

CHAPTER 3

1. Andrew Root, *The Pastor in a Secular Age: Ministry to People Who No Longer Need a God* (Grand Rapids: Baker Academic, 2019), 168.

2. Kevin J. Vanhoozer and Owen Strachan, *The Pastor as Public Theologian: Reclaiming a Lost Vision* (Grand Rapids: Baker Academic, 2015), 7.

3. While this quotation is widely attributed to Keller on the Internet, I have been unable to confirm the original source from which it comes.

4. Maryanne Wolf, *Reader, Come Home: The Reading Brain in a Digital World* (New York: HarperCollins, 2018), 198.

5. Fleming Rutledge, interview with Garrett Brown, *New Books in Biblical Studies*, podcast audio, September 13, 2016, https://newbooksnetwork.com/fleming-rutledge-the-crucifixion-understanding-the-death-of-jesus-christ-eerdmans-2015.

6. C. S. Lewis, "On the Reading of Old Books," in *God in the Dock: Essays on Theology and Ethics* (Grand Rapids: Eerdmans, 1970), 200–207.

CHAPTER 4

1. M. Craig Barnes, *The Pastor as Minor Poet: Texts and Subtexts in the Ministerial Life* (Grand Rapids: Eerdmans, 2009), 48–53.

2. M. Craig Barnes, *Diary of a Pastor's Soul: The Holy Moments in a Life of Ministry* (Grand Rapids: Brazos, 2020), 11–13.

3. Barnes, *The Pastor as Minor Poet*, 49.

4. Eugene H. Peterson, *Under the Unpredictable Plant: An Exploration in Vocational Holiness* (Grand Rapids: Eerdmans, 1992), 20.

5. Eugene H. Peterson, *The Contemplative Pastor: Returning to the Art of Spiritual Direction* (Grand Rapids: Eerdmans, 1989), 18.

6. Eugene H. Peterson, *The Pastor: A Memoir* (New York: HarperOne, 2011), 156–58.

7. Maryanne Wolf, *Reader, Come Home: The Reading Brain in a Digital World* (New York: HarperCollins, 2018), 192.

8. David Brooks, "History for Dollars," *New York Times*, June 7, 2010, https://www.nytimes.com/2010/06/08/opinion/08brooks.html.

9. George Eliot, *Middlemarch* (New York: New American Library, 1964), 811.

CHAPTER 5

1. Miroslav Volf, *Exclusion and Embrace: A Theological Exploration of Identity, Otherness, and Reconciliation* (Nashville: Abingdon, 1996), 39–40.

2. Volf, *Exclusion and Embrace*, 49.

3. Maryanne Wolf, *Proust and the Squid* (New York: HarperCollins, 2007), 7.

4. Quoted in Maryanne Wolf, *Reader, Come Home: The Reading Brain in a Digital World* (New York: HarperCollins, 2018), 43. Here, Wolf also cites Dunne as writing, "Passing over [through reading] is an equal and opposite process of *coming back* to oneself," which Wolf claims "is a beautifully apt description for how we move from our inherently circumscribed views of the world to enter another's and return enlarged."

5. Wolf, *Reader, Come Home*, 44.

6. Alan Jacobs, *A Theology of Reading: The Hermeneutics of Love* (Boulder, CO: Westview, 2001), 119.

7. Wolf, *Reader, Come Home*, 47.

CHAPTER 6

1. Cornelius Plantinga Jr., *Reading for Preaching: The Preacher in Conversation with Storytellers, Biographers, Poets, and Journalists* (Grand Rapids: Eerdmans, 2013), 6.

2. Walter Brueggemann, *Finally Comes the Poet: Daring Speech for Proclamation* (Minneapolis: Fortress, 1989), 3 (emphasis added).

CHAPTER 7

1. Eugene H. Peterson, *Run with the Horses: The Quest for Life at Its Best* (Downers Grove, IL: IVP, 1983), 36.

2. Eugene H. Peterson, *Subversive Spirituality* (Grand Rapids: Eerdmans, 1997), 174–76.

3. "So we beat on, boats against the current, borne back ceaselessly into the past."

4. Charles V. Gerkin, *The Living Human Document: Re-visioning Pastoral Counseling in a Hermeneutical Mode* (Nashville: Abingdon, 1984).

5. Cornelius Plantinga Jr., *Reading for Preaching: The Preacher in Conversation with Storytellers, Biographers, Poets, and Journalists* (Grand Rapids: Eerdmans, 2013), 7 (emphasis added).

CHAPTER 8

1. James K. A. Smith, *Imagining the Kingdom: How Worship Works* (Grand Rapids: Baker Academic, 2013), 101–91.

2. Jürgen Moltmann, *The Church in the Power of the Spirit* (Minneapolis: Fortress, 1993), 196 (emphasis added).

CHAPTER 9

1. Michael Hyatt, "5 Ways Reading Makes You a Better Leader," Michael Hyatt & Co., last updated January 20, 2020, https://michaelhyatt.com/science -readers-leaders/.

2. Kathleen Elkins, "Berkshire Hathaway Star Followed Warren Buffett's Advice: Read 500 Pages a Day," CNBC, March 27, 2018, https://www.cnbc.com /2018/03/27/warren-buffetts-key-tip-for-success-read-500-pages-a-day.html.

3. Alasdair MacIntyre, *After Virtue: A Study in Moral Theory* (Notre Dame: University of Notre Dame Press, 1981), 8.

CHAPTER 10

1. Quoted in Maryanne Wolf, *Reader, Come Home: The Reading Brain in a Digital World* (New York: HarperCollins, 2018), 46.

2. Alan Jacobs, *The Pleasures of Reading in an Age of Distraction* (New York: Oxford University Press, 2011), 67.

Notes

3. Eugene H. Peterson, *The Contemplative Pastor: Returning to the Art of Spiritual Direction* (Grand Rapids: Eerdmans, 1989), 23.

CHAPTER 11

1. See Charles Duhigg, *The Power of Habit: Why We Do What We Do in Life and Business* (New York: Random House, 2014), for a helpful and accessible overview. Duhigg talks specifically about "keystone habits" in the prologue.

2. Richard J. Foster, *Celebration of Discipline: The Path to Spiritual Growth* (New York: HarperOne, 2018).

3. Henri Nouwen, *Spiritual Direction: Wisdom for the Long Walk of Faith* (New York: HarperCollins, 2006), 64–66.

4. Dallas Willard, *The Spirit of the Disciplines: Understanding How God Changes Lives* (New York: HarperOne, 1995).

5. Duhigg, *The Power of Habit*, xvi.

CHAPTER 12

1. Owen Flanagan, *The Problem of the Soul: Two Visions of Mind and How to Reconcile Them* (New York: Basic Books, 2002), 11.

2. Krista Tippett, interview with Miroslav Volf, *For the Life of the World*, podcast audio, March 6, 2021, https://podcasts.apple.com/us/podcast/for -the-life-of-the-world-yale-center-for-faith-culture/id1505076294.

3. Alan Jacobs, *A Theology of Reading: The Hermeneutics of Love* (Boulder, CO: Westview, 2001), 81.

4. Quoted in Alan Jacobs, *The Pleasures of Reading in an Age of Distraction* (New York: Oxford University Press, 2011), 53.

5. Quoted in Jacobs, *The Pleasures of Reading*, 92.

CHAPTER 13

1. Alan Jacobs, *The Pleasures of Reading in an Age of Distraction* (New York: Oxford University Press, 2011). See particularly pp. 23–34.

2. James K. A. Smith, *Imagining the Kingdom: How Worship Works* (Grand Rapids: Baker Academic, 2013), 133.

3. See C. S. Lewis, *God in the Dock: Essays on Theology and Ethics* (Grand Rapids: Eerdmans, 1970), 65–66.

4. See "Reading Habits of Today's Pastors," Barna, June 3, 2013, https://

www.barna.com/research/reading-habits-of-todays-pastors/. See also Jackson W. Carroll, *God's Potters: Pastoral Leadership and the Shaping of Congregations* (Grand Rapids: Eerdmans, 2006), 108–10.

CHAPTER 14

1. See "How People Read Content Online—Statistics and Trends," GO-Gulf, June 25, 2018, https://www.go-gulf.ae/how-people-read-content-online/. See also Nicholas Carr, *The Shallows: What the Internet Is Doing to Our Brains* (New York: Norton, 2011), and Maryanne Wolf, *Reader, Come Home: The Reading Brain in a Digital World* (New York: HarperCollins, 2018).

2. Carr, *The Shallows*, 9.

3. Carr, *The Shallows*, 10.

4. Eugene H. Peterson, *The Contemplative Pastor: Returning to the Art of Spiritual Direction* (Grand Rapids: Eerdmans, 1989), 24.

5. What follows will deal strictly with the marking and filing of tangible reading materials. Everything described here, though, can be adapted to and performed on a portable reader.

CHAPTER 15

1. Richard Hays, *Echoes of Scripture in the Letters of Paul* (New Haven: Yale University Press, 1989), 16.

2. N. T. Wright, *Paul: A Biography* (New York: HarperOne, 2018), 16.

3. Richard Hays, *Reading Backwards* (Waco, TX: Baylor University Press, 2014), 104.

4. Cornelius Plantinga Jr., *Reading for Preaching: The Preacher in Conversation with Storytellers, Biographers, Poets, and Journalists* (Grand Rapids: Eerdmans, 2013), 9–10.

5. Alan Jacobs, *A Theology of Reading: The Hermeneutics of Love* (Boulder, CO: Westview, 2001), 111.

6. Leland Ryken, *How to Read the Bible as Literature . . . and Get More out of It* (Grand Rapids: Zondervan, 1984), 12.

7. Wright, *Paul*, 16–17.

8. 2 Timothy 4:9a, 13 NRSV. For clarity's sake, I have condensed verse 13, which in full reads: "When you come, bring the cloak that I left with Carpus at Troas, also the books, and above all the parchments."

Index

Index

INDEX

winter relief ministry, 46–47, 81–83, 87–88

wisdom, 16, 32, 34, 40–41, 48–49

Wolf, Maryanne, 16–17, 20–21, 34, 49, 53, 55, 56, 59

Wolff, Michael, 30

wonder, sense of, 148–49

Woolf, Virginia, 71

Wright, N. T., 82, 145–46, 147, 150

writing, sermons, 67–68

You Are What You Love: The Spiritual Power of Habit (Smith), 18